Understanding Contemporary American Literature
Matthew J. Bruccoli, Series Editor

Volumes on

Albee • Nicholson Baker • John Barth • Donald Barthelme
The Beats • The Black Mountain Poets • Robert Bly
Raymond Carver • Fred Chappel • Chicano Literature
Contemporary American Drama
Contemporary American Horror Fiction
Contemporary American Literary Theory
Contemporary American Science Fiction
Comtemporary Chicana Literature
Dickey • E. L. Doctorow • John Gardner • George Garrett
Hawkes • Joseph Heller • Lillian Hellman • John Irving
Randall Jarrell • William Kennedy • Jack Kerouac
la K. Le Guin • Denise Levertov • Bernard Malamud
bie Ann Mason • Jill McCorkle • Carson McCullers
S. Merwin • Arthur Miller • Toni Morrison's Fiction
dimir Nabokov • Gloria Naylor • Joyce Carol Oates
m O'Brien • Flannery O'Connor • Cynthia Ozick
ker Percy • Katherine Anne Porter • Reynolds Price
nie Proulx • Thomas Pynchon • Theodore Roethke
Philip Roth • Hubert Selby, Jr. • Mary Lee Settle
aac Bashevis Singer • Jane Smiley • Gary Snyder
William Stafford • Anne Tyler • Kurt Vonnegut
bert Penn Warren • James Welch • Eudora Welty
Tennessee Williams • August Wilson

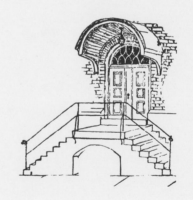

UNDERSTA

ANNIE P

Edward

F

James
John

Ursu
Bo
W.
Vla
T
Wa
Ar

Is

Ro

UNDERSTANDING
ANNIE
PROULX

Karen L. Rood

University of South Carolina Press

UNIVERSITY OF SOUTH CAROLINA *BICENTENNIAL*

© 2001 University of South Carolina

Published in Columbia, South Carolina, by the
University of South Carolina Press

Manufactured in the United States of America

05   04   03   02   01   5   4   3   2   1

Library of Congress Cataloging-in-Publication Data

Rood, Karen Lane.
    Understanding Annie Proulx / Karen L. Rood.
      p. cm. — (Understanding contemporary American literature)
    Includes bibliographical references (p.) and index.
    ISBN 1-57003-402-8 (cloth : alk. paper)
    1. Proulx, Annie—Criticism and interpretation. 2. Women and
literature—United States—History—20th century. 3. Regionalism
in literature. I. Title. II. Series.
PS3566.R697 Z86   2001
813'.54—dc21   00-012563

For Nelson Magruder Rood
and
Benjamin Armstrong Rood

CONTENTS

EDITOR'S PREFACE

The volumes of *Understanding Contemporary American Literature* have been planned as guides or companions for students as well as good nonacademic readers. The editor and publisher perceive a need for these volumes because much of the influential contemporary literature makes special demands. Uninitiated readers encounter difficulty in approaching works that depart from the traditional forms and techniques of prose and poetry. Literature relies on conventions, but the conventions keep evolving; new writers form their own conventions—which in time may become familiar. Put simply, *UCAL* provides instruction in how to read certain contemporary writers— identifying and explicating their material, themes, use of language, point of view, structures, symbolism, and responses to experience.

The word *understanding* in the titles was deliberately chosen. Many willing readers lack an adequate understanding of how contemporary literature works; that is, what the author is attempting to express and the means by which it is conveyed. Although the criticism and analysis in the series have been aimed at a level of general accessibility, these introductory volumes are meant to be applied in conjunction with the works they cover. They do not provide a substitute for the works and authors they introduce, but rather prepare the reader for more profitable literary experiences.

M. J. B.

UNDERSTANDING
ANNIE PROULX

CHAPTER ONE

Understanding Annie Proulx

Annie Proulx achieved renown as a fiction writer relatively late in life, when her first novel, *Postcards* (1992), earned her the 1993 PEN/Faulkner Award. More honors followed for her second novel, *The Shipping News* (1993), which won a National Book Award for Fiction, a *Chicago Tribune* Heartland Prize for Fiction, and an *Irish Times* International Fiction Prize in 1993, as well as the Pulitzer Prize for Fiction in 1994. The novel became a best-seller, earning Proulx, at fifty-eight, a reputation as an important "new" fiction writer. Proulx, however, had been writing short fiction for magazines since the 1950s and had been supporting herself and her three sons as a writer of mostly nonfiction since the mid-1970s, polishing the distinctive prose style that eventually brought her acclaim. Though her first four works of fiction were published under the name E. Annie Proulx, she announced in 1997 that she would prefer to be known as Annie Proulx and would use that name on all future writings.

The daughter of George Napoleon Proulx and Lois "Nellie" Gill Proulx, Edna Annie Proulx was born in Norwich, Connecticut, on 22 August 1935, the eldest of five daughters. (Her last name is pronounced "pru.") Her mother's family, the Gills, emigrated from the west of England to New England in 1635. Two years later, the Proulxs left France for Quebec. In the 1860s her father's grandparents immigrated to New England to find employment in the textile mills. Proulx's father also worked in that industry, eventually becoming a company vice president and traveling to South America and Russia as a textile expert.[1] Proulx credits her mother, an artist and amateur naturalist whose family had "a strong tradition of oral storytelling," with teaching her "to see and appreciate the natural world, to develop an eye for detail, and to tell a story."[2]

Because of George Proulx's job, the family moved frequently during her childhood, living in towns in Vermont, North Carolina, Maine, and Rhode Island. Annie Proulx attended a one-room school in Brookfield, Vermont, Black Mountain High School in North Carolina, and Deering High School in Portland, Maine, before enrolling at Colby College in Waterville, Maine, in the class of 1957.[3]

Before earning her degree, Proulx dropped out of Colby and married H. Ridgely Bullock Jr. in 1955. They were divorced in 1960, and their daughter, Sylvia Marion, was brought up by her father. Several years later Proulx married again. Two sons, Jonathan Edward and Gillis Crowell, were born of this marriage, which also ended in divorce. In 1963 Proulx returned to Vermont and went back to school. She earned a B.A. cum laude in history at the University of Vermont in Burlington in 1969. In that year she married James Hamilton Lang, who adopted her children from her second marriage. Lang is the father of Proulx's third son, Morgan Hamilton. This marriage also ended in divorce.[4]

After graduating from the University of Vermont, Proulx attended graduate school in history at Sir George Williams University (now Concordia University) in Montreal. She earned an M.A. in 1973 and then did doctoral work in Renaissance economic history, passing her oral examinations in 1975. As Proulx told an interviewer in 1999, during graduate school she was "attracted to the French *Annales* school, which pioneered minute examination of the lives of ordinary people through account books, wills, marriage and death records, farming and crafts techniques, the development of technologies."[5] Rejecting the narrow definition of history as a record of the political and military activities of so-called great men, these historians look at the evolution of everyday life in the context of larger social, economic, and even geological change.[6] Proulx's statement that she is "keenly interested in situations of change, both personal and social"[7] and her focus in her fiction on individuals living in periods of major social and economic upheaval demonstrate the extent to which her academic training has shaped the course of her career as a novelist.

Proulx had begun writing short stories for magazines before she entered Sir George Williams University. Each year she was in graduate school, from 1970 through 1974, *Seventeen,* which first published a story by Proulx in 1964, took one or two of her stories. These stories are written for a teenage audience and address subjects commonly found in such fiction—such as popularity, social values, and self-awareness. Yet some of the themes of Proulx's mature fiction are already apparent. Her first *Seventeen* story, "All the Pretty Little Horses" (June 1964), and her last, "The Yellow Box" (December 1974), both emphasize the value of understanding the past and preserving one's heritage. "All the Pretty Little Horses" also introduces the ecological concerns that run throughout Proulx's fiction for adults. "The Ugly Room" (August 1972) and "Yellow-Leaves" (April 1974) are about teenage girls growing up among the rural poor of New England, the focus of the adult short stories collected in Proulx's first book, *Heart Songs and Other Stories* (1988), and of her first novel, *Postcards.*

In 1975 Proulx decided against a career in teaching and dropped out of graduate school. Living with a friend in Canaan, Vermont, in the area of the state known as the Northeast Kingdom,

Proulx found few employment opportunities in this rural area near the Canadian border and turned to freelance journalism to support herself and her three sons. For more than a decade she wrote articles on subjects including fishing, black flies, apples, cidermaking, canoeing, mountain lions, gardening, and cooking for magazines such as *Gourmet, Horticulture, Gray's Sporting Journal, Blair and Ketchums, Outdoor Life, National Wildlife, Organic Gardening,* and *Country Journal.* After a few years she was writing nonfiction on assignment for magazines and "scribbling away on short stories" when she had time.[8] The majority of her fiction during this period was published in *Gray's Sporting Journal,* a magazine with high literary standards for the outdoor stories it publishes. In 1999 Proulx recalled the "intense camaraderie and shared literary excitement among the writers whose fiction appeared in *Gray's.*" Without this experience, she asserted, she "would probably never have tried to write fiction."[9]

Proulx also wrote nonfiction books and pamphlets. In 1980 and 1981 she wrote pamphlets on making apple cider, growing grapes, making insulated window shutters, and practicing the art of barter for the Garden Way how-to series. She and a friend, Lew Nichols, wrote two full-length books, *Sweet and Hard Cider: Making It, Using It, and Enjoying It* (1980) for Garden Way and *The Complete Dairy Foods Cookbook* (1982) for Rodale Press. In 1983 she moved to Vershire, Vermont, where she founded and edited a small monthly newspaper, *The Vershire Behind the Times* (1984–1986).

Proulx subsequently wrote three more books for Rodale Press: *The Gardener's Journal and Record Book* (1983), *Plan and Make Your Own Fences and Gates, Walkways, Walls, and Drives* (1983), and *The Fine Art of Salad Gardening* (1985). She also wrote *The*

Gourmet Gardener (1987) for Fawcett Columbine. She "made a very decent living writing books on rural affairs for hire for Rodale Press" along with the nonfiction articles and short stories she sold to magazines.[10]

Proulx dismisses her nonfiction books, which are now in demand among book collectors, as assignments for hire that she wrote to earn money. Like most how-to books and cookbooks they were not widely reviewed. Yet brief notices in periodicals such as *Publishers Weekly, Booklist,* and *Library Journal* praised their thoroughness and usefulness to the general reader, and Proulx won a Garden Writers of America Award in 1986.

For the student of Proulx's later fiction her nonfiction is interesting for the historical perspective that she often brings to her subjects. For example, the reader finds histories of cider and the dairy in the books she wrote with Nichols, and *The Gardener's Journal and Record Book* is illustrated with engravings from nineteenth-century garden books "because they instruct and inform us with a richness of detail sadly absent in our own gardening works."[11] *Plan and Make Your Own Fences and Gates, Walkways, Walls, and Drives* is particularly interesting for its histories of early American fences, stone walls, and brickmaking. It also includes an anecdote about late-twentieth-century articles in popular periodicals that mistakenly identify root cellars built in hillsides "by great-great-grandfather to store his turnips" as ancient Celtic or Phoenician structures. Similar examples of such "Modern ignorance"[12] appear in *Postcards* and "Electric Arrows," a short story collected in *Heart Songs and Other Stories.*

Like Proulx's nonfiction, her fiction is based on extensive research, which has contributed to the wealth of detail that reviewers have often praised in her fictional style. Information about what people eat, how it is prepared, and how cooking has changed over time is threaded through her fiction, adding depth to characterization and supporting social commentary. Her fascination with this important aspect of everyday life is apparent in Proulx's nonfiction books and articles on food, including fascinating accounts such as "The Curious, the Bizarre, the Delectable, and the Impossible" (*Gray's Sporting Journal,* September 1978), in which Proulx and Nichols describe how many varieties of game birds were cooked and eaten from ancient times through the first half of the twentieth century, and "North Woods Provender" (*Gourmet,* November 1979), in which Proulx describes dishes that have been served in the lumber camps of northern New England, Quebec, and New Brunswick for two centuries and traces their roots to the cooking of French Canadians of Norman ancestry.

During the years in which she made a living from writing nonfiction, Proulx at first sold her short stories mainly to sporting and outdoor magazines, but in 1982 her fiction reached a national audience of general readers when Tom Jenks accepted "The Wer-Trout" for the June issue of *Esquire.* He accepted two additional stories for the magazine before taking a job with Charles Scribner's Sons and inviting Proulx to collect some of her short stories into a book.[13]

The result was *Heart Songs and Other Stories,* published in October 1988. The reviews were mostly the sort of brief comments typically accorded a collection of short fiction by a little-known author, but they were on the whole laudatory. The *Publishers Weekly* reviewer called Proulx "a writer to watch" (19 August 1988), while Kenneth Rosen, writing for the "In Short" column of the *New York Times Book Review* (29 January 1989) praised her "sometimes enigmatic, often lyrical images."[14]

Proulx's contract with Scribners included a novel. Thinking of herself as a short-story writer, Proulx was at first uncertain that she would be able to write a longer work of fiction, but once she started writing *Postcards,* she found the process easier than writing short fiction. A publisher's advance and grants from the Vermont Council on the Arts in 1989 and the Ucross Foundation in 1990 allowed her to devote herself to fiction writing for the first time in her life. She drove cross-country "several times to catch the unfolding of the landscape and translate it into the vanished landscape of the 1940s and '50s."[15] She wrote *Postcards* in 1990, during a six-week residency at the Ucross Foundation in Clearmont, Wyoming, in the foothills of the Big Horn Mountains. She found that she could write easily there and wrote her next two novels at the foundation as well.

Published in January 1992, *Postcards* met with positive reviews. Writing about three first novels in *Chicago Tribune Books* (12 January 1992), novelist Frederick Busch devoted more than an equally apportioned amount of space to *Postcards,* describing it as more like a fifth or sixth novel than a first attempt and calling Proulx a "richly talented writer."[16] In the *New York Times Book Review* (22 March 1992), David Bradley went even further than Busch in his praise, saying the Proulx had "come close" to achieving the impossible goal of writing the Great American Novel: that is, a novel epitomizing the American experience as a whole.[17]

Published in March 1993, Proulx's second novel, *The Shipping News,* is set in Newfoundland, which Proulx visited for the first time in the mid-1980s during a fishing trip with a friend.[18] She later bought a house on the Great Northern Peninsula of the island and spends time there each year. By the time she completed *The Shipping News* with the help of a grant from the National Endowment for the Arts in 1991 and a Guggenheim Fellowship in 1992, she had made nine trips to the island, "watching, observing, taking notes and listening."[19] Filled with closely observed details of Newfoundland life and language, *The Shipping News* won the enthusiastic praise of critics and became a best-seller. The novelist Sandra Scofield, writing in the *Washington Post Book World* (1 August 1993), described it as "a novel that reinvents the tale and gives us a hero for our times."[20] In *Chicago Tribune Books* (29 March 1993) Stephen Jones called the novel "a lyric page turner,"[21] and Howard Norman, writing for the *New York Times Book Review,* praised Proulx's "surreal humor and her zest for the strange foibles of humanity."[22] The most accessible of Proulx's novels, *The Shipping News* was also her most widely acclaimed, bringing her four major awards.

Proulx has recounted that she developed the idea for her next novel, *Accordion Crimes,* while she was still writing *The Shipping News,* as she "sat shaking and aching in the middle of the night in the hours after a bite by a Brown Recluse spider." She used that experience in the third section of *Accordion Crimes,* which is set in Texas and is the only part of the original draft she included in the final version. At first her plan was for the entire story of an accordion passing from one immigrant group to another to be set in Texas, "a state with an extremely rich immigrant population," but after she did not receive a hoped-for residency fellowship that would have allowed her to spend six months in Texas fitting her plotline into the landscape of the state, she had to rethink the book. The result was much more ambitious than her original plan: an attempt to define the entire American "immigrant experience and the individual and cultural costs of abandoning the past and reinventing oneself."[23]

With eight sets of characters spread over more than a century and a wide range of locations, the novel is more epic in scope and less tightly structured than Proulx's first two novels. Some critics were bothered by the bigger and looser structure, and the reviewer for the influential *New York Times Book Review* (23 June 1996) disliked the frequent depictions of violence in the novel. As Proulx commented in 1999, it is hard to take seriously criticism of the violence in her fiction. After all, "America is a violent, gun-handling country." Adding that in most cases the violence suffered by her characters is "drawn from true accounts of public record," she explained that her characters' "bitter deaths and misadventures . . . illustrate American violence which is real, deep and vast."[24] Other reviewers, including the critics for the *Washington Post Book World* (16 June 1996) and *Chicago Tribune Books* (9 June 1996), praised *Accordion Crimes,* and John Sutherland wrote in the *New Republic* (7 October 1996), that while *The Shipping News* demonstrated that Proulx is "a good novelist," *Accordion Crimes* revealed that she is "a great novelist."[25]

In 1995 Proulx moved to Wyoming, where she now makes her home, though she spends much of each year traveling. In Wyoming, she writes, "[t]he long sight-lines encourage clarity of vision, the roll of high plains and stony steeps satisfy some inner longings smothered by my native New England woods."[26] The stories in her 1999 book, *Close Range: Wyoming Stories,* demonstrate the depth to which she has come to understand her new home and its history. The *New York Times* reviewer Christopher Lehmann-Haupt, who had mixed feelings about *Accordion Crimes,* admired the "wry poetry of loneliness and pain" in Proulx's Wyoming stories (12 May 1999) while Richard Eder, writing for the *New York Times Book Review* (23 May 1999), admired Proulx's "feeling for place and the shape into which it twists her characters." John Skow wrote an enthusiastic appreciation of Proulx's language for *Time* (17 May 1999).[27]

The overarching concern of Proulx's fiction is the way in which ordinary people conduct their lives in the face of social, economic, and ecological change. From *Heart Songs and Other Stories,* with its focus on the interactions of the rural poor and the city people who are gradually buying up their land, and *Postcards,* which depicts the decline of the small New England family farm in the period of accelerated urbanization that began during the Second World War, Proulx went on, in *The Shipping News,* to show how the intrusion of modernization and big government is gradually destroying a traditional way of life in Newfoundland. Taking on the American melting-pot mentality that expected immigrants to give up the cultures of their homelands in order to gain acceptance, *Accordion Crimes* covers roughly a century of American life, from the 1890s to the 1990s. It looks at the people left behind in the rush toward "modernity" and the American Dream of prosperity. In *Close Range* Proulx illustrates the plight of Wyoming ranchers succumbing to the same general forces of modernization and big government as the New England farmers and Newfoundland fisherman in her earlier fiction.

Ever since the publication of *Postcards*—a novel about a man who murders his fiancée and wastes his life on the run, simultaneously obsessed with guilt and self-justification—reviewers have compared Proulx's fiction to that of Frank Norris and Theodore Dreiser. *Postcards* has a thematic connection to Norris's *McTeague*

(1898), in which the title character kills his wife, and Dreiser's *An American Tragedy* (1925), about a young man who kills his fiancée. Yet Proulx goes beyond the old-fashioned genetic and social determinism that lies at the heart of these novels. Though nature and nurture are factors in her characters' fates, she expresses a more complex view of the forces that influence their lives. "Geography, geology, climate, weather, the deep past, immediate events, shape the characters and partly determine what happens to them," she explained in 1999, "although the random event counts for much as it does in life," and her characters "pick their way through the chaos of change." The world of Proulx's fiction offers no certainty, for good or for ill. Yet regardless of the hardships her characters encounter, Proulx notes, they harbor "the images of an ideal and seemingly attainable world." She reveals in her fiction "the historical skew between what people have hoped for and who they thought they were and what befell them."[28]

A closer antecedent of Proulx's fiction is the early fiction of John Dos Passos, with its focus on the ordinary, working-class American trying to cope in an increasingly urban and industrialized capitalist society during the first half of the twentieth century. The broad canvasses of *Postcards* and *Accordion Crimes* may be considered attempts to define the American experience for Proulx's generation in the same way that Dos Passos's *U.S.A.* trilogy (1930–1936) forced his contemporaries to take a critical look at the American Dream.

Proulx admires her characters' traditional lifestyles and is well know for weaving information about topics such as language, customs, food, and craftsmanship into her narratives. She has been widely recognized for her lyrical prose style, her ability to create strikingly original images to express stark, sometimes horrifying truths. She is also well known for her wry humor, which often lightens the mood of violent scenes and pessimistic observations on human nature. Though she doe not wholly dismiss the redemptive power of love or the possibility of selfless actions, she more often than not portrays human beings as motivated by selfish concerns, showing how insecurity and hurt tend to spawn not compassion but anger, hatred, prejudice, and violence.

Proulx's intermixture of the humorous with the horrific bears comparison to Flannery O'Connor's. Yet, for O'Connor, a devout Roman Catholic, her bizarre characters and frequent use of violence were part of an attempt to show her readers how far the modern world has strayed from true Christianity. She had fixed religious and moral standards against which to measure human actions. Because Proulx's world of shifting values has no such guideposts, it is a more frightening place than O'Connor's world. The most humorous and most grotesque caricatures in O'Connor's fiction are individuals who have unwittingly or willfully fallen away from God's grace and become agents of the devil. According to Proulx, she creates her characters "to carry a particular story." She refuses to "give them their heads and 'see where they go.'" Yet her characters are complex beings, and she adds that the "work of inventing a believable and fictionally 'true' person on paper is exhilarating, particularly as one knowingly skates near the thin ice of caricature."[29] In their roles of carrying the plotline Proulx's characters sometimes become what may be called secular versions of O'Connor's grotesques. The most extreme of them become so obsessed with their emotional scars that they gradually turn into little more than personifications of single overwhelming emotions. Because they are more complex and their emotional deformities have different, and more varied, roots than those of O'Connor's apostates, Proulx's grotesques also have more varied fates. Some, including Quoyle in *The Shipping News* and Ottaline in "The Bunchgrass Edge of the World" (1998), who both feel like outsiders because of their huge bodies, become progressively less grotesque as they discover possibilities for human relationships. Others, such as Rivers in "The Wer-Trout" (1982), Hans Beutle in *Accordion Crimes,* and Car Scope in "The Governors of Wyoming" (1999), are seriocomic. The reader recognizes their self-inflicted plights but is too amused by their folly to feel much sympathy. Hawkheel in "On the Antler" (1983), Mme Malefoot in *Accordion Crimes,* and Mero in "The Half-Skinned Steer" (1997) are among the characters who, more pathetic than funny, nonetheless elicit laughter at their single-minded obsessions. Some characters, including Dub Blood in *Postcards* and Howard Poplin and Ivar Gasmann in *Accordion Crimes* are less-than-admirable comic grotesques who experience undeserved successes, while purely pathetic grotesques, such as Vela Gasmann in *Accordion Crimes,* are doomed to unhappiness. Proulx's most grotesque character is the murderer Loyal Blood in *Postcards,* who deserves his fate but still draws reader sympathy because of Proulx's ability to describe his complex feelings of anger, self-justification, and guilt.

Just as Proulx's characters can become exaggerated versions of real people, her plotlines are occasionally interrupted by excursions into magical realism, a technique in which a plausible narrative enters the realm of fantasy without establishing a clearly defined line between the possible and impossible. Though Proulx often gives the reader "realistic" explanations for bizarre happenings, sometimes she purposely leaves such puzzles unresolved.

Proulx rarely uses first-person narration. Only three of her collected stories—"Stone City" and "Electric Arrows" in *Heart Songs and Other Stories* and "A Lonely Coast" in *Close Range: Wyoming Stories*—are narrated from a first-person point of view. The rest of her collected stories and all three of her novels are narrated from third-person-limited perspectives that, particularly in the novels and sometimes in her longer stories, shift from character to character to present more than one point of view. Through this technique, complications in a plotline are usually revealed gradually. Though the time span of the novel or short story proceeds in a linear fashion, important events of the past, and further information about episodes that have occurred earlier in the novel, are revealed as they come to a character's mind, or as a character learns more about them. Thus, Proulx's stories tend to have a thematic, rather than chronological, order. Her third-person narrators often comment on the action, usually paraphrasing or summarizing a character's thoughts rather than interjecting an authorial viewpoint. Sometimes, however, Proulx's narrators do step out of character to offer an authorial perspective, and in *Accordion Crimes* she uses this point of view in a technique she calls the "flash-forward" to reveal what happens to a character outside the time frame of the novel.

Proulx's fiction may be seen as part of a late twentieth-century trend toward a new regionalism. While southern regional writing has always remained strong, in the early years of the century the sophisticated, dispassionate writings of the great modernists made the local-color stories of other regions—so popular at the end of the previous century—seem poorly crafted and overly sentimental. At the same time, as Americans became increasingly urban, critics began to dismiss such rural fiction as irrelevant and outmoded. By the 1980s, however, this trend seemed to be reversing, with critical praise, literary prizes, and best-seller status accorded not only to Proulx's novels but to other notable works such as Carolyn Chute's *The Beans of Egypt, Maine* (1985), set in rural New England; John Casey's *Spartina* (1989), set in coastal Rhode Island; and Cormac McCarthy's *All the Pretty Horses* (1992), the first volume of this trilogy set on both sides of the U.S.–Mexican border. Like Proulx, these writers have learned not only from the modernists, but also from the magical realists and the minimalists—writers such as Raymond Carver and Ann Beattie, who trace their understated style to Ernest Hemingway—embracing some lessons while rejecting others. Readers who approach the works of these new regionalists out of a turn-of-the-century nostalgia for getting back to their country roots quickly have their notions of pastoral serenity replaced by pictures of rural poverty and varying degrees of violence. Proulx is the most ambitious of these writers, not only in her broad focus on more than one region but also in her attempt to explore the underlying causes of the social ills she depicts. As she told the *Missouri Review* interviewer in 1999, "The novel should take us, as readers, to a vantage point from which we can confront our human condition" and "see ourselves as living entities in the jammed and complex contemporary world."[30]

CHAPTER TWO

Heart Songs and Other Stories

The nine stories in the first edition of *Heart Songs and Other Stories* (1988)—as well as the two stories added to the 1995 edition—are set during the second half of the twentieth century in areas of northern New England where great natural beauty exists alongside grinding rural poverty. As the small dairy farms that had been the basis for the regional economy began to fail after the Second World War, wealthy outsiders began to buy old family farms for vacation or retirement homes. While many of the descendants of the farmers who tilled the land since colonial days left in search of work in urban areas, others stayed on, living in battered trailers and rundown houses. They survived by farming the small plots of land that were left to them, by accepting welfare, or by working at scarce low-paying service jobs— often working for the new owners of ancestral lands. Only traces remain of a traditional agrarian society in which people lived by the fruits of their labor and with the assistance of an interdependent network of family and neighbors, understanding and revering the natural surroundings from which they drew their sustenance.

When the title story was published in the October 1986 issue of *Esquire,* the magazine included a statement from novelist Mary Lee Settle that characterizes Proulx's accomplishment not just in that story but in her first book as a whole: "Annie Proulx's work is as real as a pickup truck, as ominous as a fairy tale. She knows about men and women and woods and animals and the thousand natural shocks that flesh is heir to. She writes sensuously about the country, but she is not a 'nature' writer. She catches the frightening undertow of the backwoods and its people, but she does not romanticize or judge or stoop to sensation. She ignores fashion in favor of a true voice and vision. She haunts."[1]

Proulx's knowledge of country ways, gleaned through meticulous reading and research as well as her firsthand experience of living in northern Vermont, is apparent throughout the stories. Readers can, for example, extract a bibliography of classic outdoorsman's books from "On the Antler"; discover something about the behavioral patterns of foxes in "Stone City"; learn a bit about the lore of deer hunting, methods of rural road construction, and making steamed brown bread on a woodstove in "A Run of Bad Luck"; and find a list of old varieties of apples in "Electric Arrows."

Lacking knowledge of the ways and the history of the country people they are displacing, the outsiders in these stories are frequently sources of humor as they misinterpret and misjudge the actions and motives of rural individuals who are more attuned to the cycle of the seasons and steeped in a way of life alien to city dwellers. All but two of the stories in the collection include outsiders who misunderstand their country neighbors.

Yet, for all their knowledge of the land and how to live on it, Proulx's rural characters are not idealized as "nature's noblemen." They are not merely victims of a national market economy that has made their ways of earning a living obsolete, or of the intrusion of influences from outsiders and the media that has weakened and in some cases destroyed aspects of traditional culture. In these stories Proulx depicts the effects of years of poverty, backbreaking work, domestic violence, incest, rape, and anger that sometimes smolders for decades before it erupts in acts of revenge. The stories often end with ironic twists of characters' expectations, for which Proulx has prepared the careful reader with earlier clues.

The nine stories in the 1988 edition are arranged thematically rather than in order of composition. The first four introduce the reader to the people who have lived in northern New England for generations, intermarrying and interacting for years, developing enmities and alliances in relative isolation—until recently—from the outside world. They are followed by stories in which well-to-do city people intrude on and upset the balance of that rural world.

"On the Antler"

Outsiders play seemingly incidental roles in "On the Antler," first published in *Harrowsmith* in 1983; yet their presence and the changes it has wrought are felt throughout the story. One of the most intense stories in the book, it is a tale of hatred and revenge, of two men made grotesque by all-consuming anger and guilt that began in their youth. The story is presented from the third-person point of view of an old man nicknamed Hawkheel. The name suggests that he is the last of the lone woodsmen, like James Fenimore Cooper's noble outdoorsman Natty Bumppo, also known as Hawkeye. Hawkheel, who represents what is likely the last generation of men steeped in the old lore of woodsmanship, bears emotional scars caused by the stigma of his father's insanity, and he is the longtime butt of the town bully's so-called jokes. Living alone in a trailer, he has gradually sold off most of his family's land in the years since his wife left him, her infidelity having been revealed by his spiteful adversary, Bill Stong. Hawkheel's one remaining source of pride is his supposedly exclusive knowledge of the best places for hunting and fishing, which he visits "like stations of the cross."[2]

Stong, the owner of the local feed store, has alienated most of the locals with his mean-spirited gossip and practical jokes. His store was ready to fail until the arrival of city people, who consider him a character and like his stories, which the townspeople recognize as untrue. To indulge the outsiders' interest in "antiques" he offers for sale the possessions of several generations of his family, "as if he had drawn a rake through their lives and piled the debris in the store" (18).

Hawkheel's hatred for Stong began during their youth: Stong told his father, the town constable and sometime truant officer, that Hawkheel was skipping school, and Hawkheel got a beating as a result. Hawkheel vowed revenge: "The game began, and the thread of rage endured like a footnote to their lives" (15).

Stong's psyche has been twisted and stunted by tragedy. Known for haphazard housekeeping, his mother cooked a pork roast in an unwashed pan that had been used to soak seed corn in strychnine in order to kill crows that ate the kernels sown in the fields. Fifteen-year-old Stong, who missed dinner because he was engaged in a youthful sexual adventure, was the only member of the family not killed by the poisoned meat. The juxtaposition of those two events causes him to connect sex and death and to avoid women. Throughout his life he remains ambivalent about his parents, alternately finding fault with them and speaking of them as saints.

As Stong continues to play mean-spirited tricks on him, Hawkheel finally finds an avenue of revenge. A dedicated reader of books on hunting, fishing, and natural history, Hawkheel has long coveted the expensive rarities he has seen in book-dealers' catalogues. Among the family possessions Stong has offered for sale,

Hawkheel finds hundreds of these valuable books, most of which Stong has priced at under two dollars. Hawkheel takes secret glee in buying the books a few at a time to avoid arousing Stong's suspicions. His fun finally ends, however, after one of the city people, a librarian, reprices the books for Stong to reflect their true value.

By this point Hawkheel is nearly consumed by anger. Not long before he discovers the books have been repriced, Hawkheel has found a faded plastic fishing bobber at one of his "secret" places, a recently discovered trout pool so high in the mountains that he had thought no white man had ever been there. Then he finds the Stong family album among the repriced books in Stong's store. In it is a photograph of Stong as a boy "trespassing" at the pool Hawkheel had not yet found. He steals the album to further contemplate Stong's "treachery" at home, and later that night he discovers that Stong has altered many of the photographs, revealing his self-loathing and guilt at surviving his family: "Over and over Stong had killed his photographic images." The album even includes Stong's "self-composed obituary" for a boy "'too bad to live' and 'hated by everybody'" (28). He listed his whole family as survivors.

Stong's tricks on Hawkheel continue. At the store he gives Hawkheel a drink of Calvados, a gift of the librarian who repriced the books. The drink makes Hawkheel too sick to go out hunting on the first day of deer season, and from his trailer he hears shots coming from his special place on Antler Mountain. Told about Hawkheel's spot by Stong, the librarian has shot a sixteen-point buck, the largest deer ever taken in the county and possibly in the state.

As "revenge" Hawkheel tears up the books he has bought from Stong and throws them at the carcass of the buck as it hangs outside Stong's store—an act that seems as self-destructive as the anger at

Stong that has filled Hawkheel's life. Yet his actions have another, more symbolic meaning as well. The way of life described in these books is fast becoming extinct. Furthermore, as the books become collectors' items rather than guides for true outdoorsmen, they come to represent just one more investment commodity in a modern capitalist economy. Hawkheel's destruction of the books may be seen as a last-ditch effort to keep the knowledge they contain away from outsiders who neither appreciate nor understand the lore of the reverent woodsman—a symbolic attempt to prevent the books from being appreciated only for their monetary value.

"Stone City"

First published in the September 1979 issue of *Gray's Sporting Journal,* "Stone City" examines several acts of revenge that have wider consequences than in "On the Antler," as the narrator, a newcomer to Chopping County, gradually comes to understand the complex interrelationships of the people in the community. He learns that the abandoned farm everyone calls Stone City was once the property of the first settlers of the county—a "real old family, and a real bad family" (47). During the lifetimes of the current residents, old man Stone was known as the "meanest bastard" and his children shared a reputation for being wild and mean. One of those children, Floyd Stone, finally brought the wrath of the community on the whole Stone family when—after waiting for a seventy-three-car train to pass—he shot and killed the man standing on the caboose. Several hundred law men converged on Stone City and tore down a flimsy house to get Floyd and arrest him. Then the locals tarred and feathered the rest of the Stone men. Old man Stone retaliated by burning out Banger, one of the leaders of the mob, killing Banger's wife and child in the process.

Floyd was eventually electrocuted, and by the time the narrator arrives in town, the Stones seem to exist only as a fearful memory. The narrator hears much of the Stones' story from Banger, a talkative man known for his skills as a hunter. He lives alone with his much-loved hunting dog and seems to have been motivated for his part in the mob by an earlier act of violence. While hunting with the narrator in the abandoned Stone City, Banger explains that he used to hunt there as a child, and that once old man Stone chased him away "with number six birdshot. Still got the little pick scars acrost my back" (40).

When Banger's dog is found dead in a trap set for foxes near Stone City, Banger blames old man Stone. In fact, the trap belongs to the son of Floyd Stone's illegitimate son, a teenager who might have found the dog in time to save it if he had tended his trapline more diligently. After Banger moves away, the narrator discovers that Banger had bought Stone City for back taxes years earlier. Still, the narrator concludes, "The Stones owned it and they always would" (53). Proulx, however, suggests the vanity of any concept of human land ownership within the larger context of geological time. The story is punctuated with a series of vignettes about a fox whose range includes Stone City. Too smart to be caught in a trap, the fox survives to father another generation in a new den built under a cellar foundation in Stone City.

"Bedrock"

In "Bedrock," one of the two stories in which outsiders play no part, the primary motivating factor is again revenge, but its presence is not fully revealed until the end of the story. A young woman, Maureen, seduces and marries Perley, a much older widower, and with the help of her brother Bobhot she proceeds to take over the running of Perley's farm, making all the decisions about crops and reducing the old man to little more than kitchen help. Perley's farm is "a thin mantle of soil that lay over bedrock scarred by glaciers and meteorites." "Atoms of this granite" course through Perley's body, but he knows that Maureen is "shot through with some wild astral substance so hard and dense that granite powdered into dust beneath her blows" (58). Knowing that he is no match for his young wife, Perley is further beaten down when he sees Bobhot and Maureen having sexual intercourse as though they have been intimate for years. He concludes that their incestuous union must have begun in their poverty-stricken childhood.

Until that point in the story Bobhot and Maureen seem to be motivated only by greed, the desire to improve their lot by acquiring a farm of their own, and Perley—who wore white when he married Maureen—seems to be the innocent victim. Yet there is one clue earlier in the story, when Maureen seduced Perley, that suggests stronger emotions lying behind their actions: "The guilty scents of willow pollen and the river in spring flooded the room, the looming shape of the past was suddenly uncovered like a hand pulled away from a face. He seemed to feel drying mud beneath his nails" (60). At the end of the story the reader learns that one spring at least ten years earlier, when he was fifty-nine and she was just a child, Perley met Maureen, her face streaked with willow pollen, by the river and raped her as she tried to escape up the muddy bank. Maureen has taken her revenge by stripping Perley's soul to its bedrock and hammering away at his granite essence with her superior hardness.

"A Run of Bad Luck"

The other story in which there are no outsiders, "A Run of Bad Luck," first published in a 1987 issue of *Ploughshares,* examines the life of a family on the eve and early morning of the first day of deer-hunting season. Despite their father's advice to the contrary, two of the four brothers, Amando and Ray, have botched a road repair because they were in a hurry, and now the county has handed Amando a bill for redoing the job that equals the family's whole profit from the original work. Amando, whose wife, Julia, has decided to divorce him, concludes that the reason for all his misfortunes is bad luck.

Later his father, Haylett, and two other brothers, Clover and Phil, discover what Amando has known already: Ray is having an affair with Amando's wife, who still retains Amando's collection of deer antlers. Amando, who has shot a deer each year since he was twelve, once told Clover that he wanted to be buried with those antlers, and Clover had imagined them buried on top of Amando "pressing him down into the yielding soil until hunter and trophies all descended to the core of the earth" (81)—a fitting image for a cuckold.

As Clover and Phil sit in the truck with their father after discovering Ray's affair with Julia, Clover refers to Amando's bad luck, but his father says luck is not involved: "It's the way his life is turning out, and he don't know it yet" (82). Sparked by his father's expression of fatalism, "Clover saw that Haylett, in begetting Amando, had created this snow-filled morning in a silent truck. A sense of the mysterious force of generation rushed in on him" (84). Throughout the story, however, there are suggestions that Amando's own decisions have also played a role in his destiny. Whatever social and economic forces shape and limit his life, it is his failure to adhere to the old ways of proper road building that has prompted the bill from the county. Yet, Amando is also one of many Proulx characters who is losing touch with old ways without connecting with the new, stuck between two cultures and benefitting from neither.

"Heart Songs"

The title story, "Heart Songs," which was included in the list of "100 Other Distinguished Short Stories of the Year 1986" in *The Best American Short Stories 1987,* introduces a theme that continues throughout the remaining five stories in the book: the outsider's misunderstanding of local ways and its sometimes serious, sometimes comic consequences. Snipe has come to Vermont with vaguely conceived get-rich-quick schemes and his girlfriend, Catherine, whose wealthy parents stand ready to help in the event of financial crisis. When Snipe begins playing music with the Twilight family in their rundown house on their mountaintop farm, he envisions record deals and easy money. Eno Twilight, the head of the family, insists, however, that the family does not perform in public, only at home in their dingy kitchen. They play their old-style country songs, arranged by Eno and fat but beautiful Nell, to "make a joyful noise unto the Lord" (93).

Snipe, who has "a secret wish to step off into some abyss of bad taste and moral sloth" (90), fails to understand the personal significance the Twilights' songs have for them and sees the family as a means to indulge his taste for the "down and dirty" (93): "He wanted fat Nell and the freedom of dirty sheets, wanted to sit in a broken chair and play music and not have to make a mark in the world"

(99). Thinking Nell is Eno's daughter, he seduces her. Then, when Eno appears and is clearly aware of what has happened, Snipe blurts out that he loves Eno's "daughter" and is told that she is his wife. Snipe flees the house with Eno in pursuit. At the end of the story Snipe is convincing Catherine that they should seek their fortune elsewhere, seemingly oblivious to the emotion damage he has inflicted on the Twilights. Like the sniper his name suggests, Snipe strikes his victims and moves on. As in Proulx's later fiction, the wealthy can easily escape situations that have become uncomfortable for them while the poor are left behind to eke out a living as best they can.

"The Unclouded Day"

In other stories outsiders are largely a source of humor. First published in the Fall 1985 issue of *Gray's Sporting Journal,* "The Unclouded Day" is in some ways typical of the sort of fiction that has been published for years in magazines for hunters and fishers, humorous stories that often feature a wily outdoorsman who gets the better of an arrogant city slicker. In Proulx's story Earl, a wealthy investment analyst who works at home in a large "Swiss chalet" with "molded polystyrene pillars holding up a portico roof" (111), hires Santee to teach him how to hunt game birds. Santee quickly decides that Earl has "the reflexes of a snowman" (111) and will never learn to shoot properly, but Earl claims to be undiscouraged. He has read in books that learning to shoot birds is a long and difficult process. Santee would like to quit, but his wife appreciates the extra money he is making.

After an entire season in which Earl has failed to shoot a single bird, Santee agrees to hunt with him for a second season because, having taken Earl's money for so long, he feels honor bound to keep hunting with him until he finally succeeds. One day, with a thunderstorm approaching, Earl wrongly believes that he has hit a bird. After Santee's dog refuses Earl's order to fetch the nonexistent bird, Santee finds three dead grouse that have just been killed when lightning struck a nearby tree. He praises Earl's supposed prowess as a hunter, and then uses Earl's criticism of the dog for not fetching the birds as an excuse to quit. Earl assumes that Santee is jealous, but Santee has the last laugh. Later that night he wonders "what Earl had said when he plucked three partridges that were already cooked" (118).

For all its humor the story also includes social commentary. Because he is paying Santee, Earl treats him like a servant. In Earl's mind this relationship allows him to imply to listeners in the general store that he has shot birds that were actually killed by Santee. Most hurtful to Santee, however, is his wife's response to Earl's wealth, and Santee comes to resent how she spends the money he earns from Earl to make their house more like the "gentrified" country homes of the city people.

"In the Pit"

Like Snipe, the outsider protagonist of "In the Pit" causes emotional pain through his misreading of others' intentions.

During a winter visit back east, Blue goes to his family's Vermont summer camp, for the first time in years, to inspect the damage done by vandals. Once there he finds some of the furnishings buried in deep snow in a pit at the base of a small cliff behind the house. Dreaming of coming to the camp in the summer with his wife and child, he reestablishes contact with Mr. Fitzroy, a dairy farmer who has been kind to Blue as a child. Fitzroy's wife has died; his house has burned down; and he has turned to drink while living in the former milk room on his farm. He does not remember Blue, but he welcomes him kindly and introduces him to Gilbert, a former convict to whom he has given shelter because, Fitzroy says, "I don't hold the past against nobody" (128).

Blue is less tolerant. After seeing what looks like his family's old toaster in Fitzroy's quarters, he accuses Gilbert of vandalizing the camp and takes the toaster by force. The next day he looks in the pit again and sees his family's toaster. The reader is left with the impression that this discovery has embarrassed Blue and probably damped his plans to vacation at the cabin, but it has contributed little to his understanding of his own character.

"The Wer-Trout"

"The Wer-Trout," first published in the June 1982 issue of *Esquire* and included in the list of "100 Other Distinguished Short Stories of the Year 1982" in *The Best American Short Stories 1983,* focuses on the self-delusions of another outsider. Rivers, whose "father's name was Riverso—Misfortune, Reverse, Wrong Side" (137), has left the city to open The March Brown, a failing shop stocked with "custom-tied flies, antique rods, imported English creels and old fishing prints, his books of Chinese poetry" (139). At the beginning of the story his wife leaves him, her exit precipitated when the woman who lives in the trailer up the road drives through their garden and mows down their little apple tree. Rivers tells himself he does not care about his wife's departure, finding peace in his Chinese poetry and the ambiance of his empty shop: "He has found a way to cure himself of all suffering and worry by memorizing ancient Chinese poems and casting artificial flies in moving water. He is solaced by the faint parallels between his own perception of events and those of the stringy-bearded scholars of the Tang, enjoying, as he does, a sad peace at the sight of feathered ephemera balanced on the dark-flowing river." (141) Realizing that all his ambition is gone, he "doesn't know if this is contentment or deadly inertia" (139).

On the same day Rivers's neighbor, Sauvage, the husband of the woman who smashed the apple tree, comes home to discover his wife eating a mouse. Because she has thrown their telephone in a sink full of hot water, Sauvage rushes to River to call an ambulance to take her to a mental hospital.

Visiting Rivers's shop the next day, Sauvage proposes a fishing trip to the Yellow Bogs in the north-country swamps, a place he has heard about from his French Canadian grandfather, who spoke of the huge brook trout to be found there. The two men set out on their adventure, which reads like a parody of Ernest Hemingway's "Big Two-Hearted River" (1925), in which Nick Adams gains a measure of psychological renewal after the trauma of the First World War.

On the trip Rivers plunges into a fantasy world of his own making. An alcoholic who has not had a drink in six years, he begins drinking heavily. While fishing apart from Sauvage, he takes off all his clothes except his boots, wades into the water, and fishes with his shirt wrapped around his head as protection against black flies. After he dresses and returns to camp, Sauvage, who has seen him through the fog but not recognized him, says there is another, crazy fisherman in the bogs. Thinking to scare Sauvage, Rivers tells him he saw the Wer-Trout (man-trout), a being with a man's body and a trout's head, who goes after fishermen who catch female trout. "[T]hat's how come our wives are gone," Rivers adds. "In the daytime when we weren't there the Wer-Trout came around . . . and scared them away" (151). Sauvage laughs off Rivers's story, but later, alone in his tent, Rivers pulls out his last bottle of whiskey and sees his face distorted in the curve of the glass, "the chinless throat, the pale snout, the vacant rusted eyes of the Wer-Trout" (152). Having become a grotesque embodiment of all the pain he has sought to avoid, he finally glimpses his own culpability in the failure of his marriage.

"Electric Arrows"

Also including humor at the expense of outsiders, "Electric Arrows" returns the focus of the book to the people whose land is being taken over. A large portion of the Clew family farm, including the original homestead, is now owned by the Moon-Azures, whose name, "blue moons," suggests their oddity in the New England landscape. A wealthy couple from Maryland, the Moon-Azures "trace Clew genealogy as though they bought our ancestors with the land" (162). Convinced that she and her husband are better able to preserve local history than those whose ancestors made it, Mrs. Moon-Azure even tries to buy a treasured collection of old family photographs from the narrator and the other remaining Clews, who live in what used to be the hired man's house and retain ownership of the barn. One day the Clews are surprised to see in a newspaper a photograph of the picture their father etched in a granite outcropping on the farm during the narrator's childhood—a primitive self-portrait of his father wearing his electric-lineman's gear and holding fanciful bolts of electricity in one hand. According to the caption in the newspaper, however, the Moon-Azures have found a "[c]omplex" petroglyph of a thunder god, "rare among the eastern woodland tribes" (169–70), a humorous instance of outsiders misinterpreting things to fit their own romanticized versions of history.

The decline of the Clew family and their neighbors, however, is not the result of the arrival of well-to-do outsiders, which is a symptom rather than a cause of the national trends that have resulted in the collapse of the local economy. Unable to compete with or understand trends in the market for farm products outside rural Vermont, the narrator's father failed as an apple farmer and went to work for the rural electric cooperative. As a farmer, he grew the varieties of apples he liked, concentrating on Baldwins when "big growers were pushing the MacIntosh and Delicious," creating a consumer demand for shiny red apples rather than the "cloudy maroon" Baldwins (158–59).

The narrator, who was always "nervy and sick," operates a small-scale electric-appliance business that his father started in the barn, where the remains of an old kite still hang on a beam. He and his sister still bear the emotional scars of childhood traumas. Their father's friend and fellow lineman, Diamond Ward, who used to slide "his old dirty paws" between the children's legs, was electrocuted while trying to retrieve a kite from an electric line, and for the rest of their childhood the children reenacted his death with that kite, taking turns playing Diamond in a mixture of vengeance and guilt.

In all nine of the stories in the 1988 edition of *Heart Songs and Other Stories* people are shaped by personal, family, and community histories, as well as larger national and international trends—

none of which they completely understand. This theme resonates throughout Proulx's novels as well, setting the stage for her attempts to come to terms with the American experience as a whole.

The two stories Proulx added to the 1995 edition of *Heart Songs and Other Stories,* published after the success of *Postcards* (1992) and *The Shipping News* (1993), return to the northern New England setting of the earlier stories.

"A Country Killing"

First published in the November 1994 issue of *Esquire,* "A Country Killing" is another story of revenge. Two Jehovah's Witnesses find Rose Noury and Warren Trussel dead in his trailer at the end of a long country road. As the story unfolds, it becomes apparent that their murderer is Rose's husband and Warren's former friend, Archie Noury, a man from a lawless and violent family, who has taken revenge for Rose's leaving him.

The story ends with the nagging uncertainty of another character, Albro Sweet, who has become obsessed with fat Rose, a woman who smells of vanilla, and has had sex with her in his truck outside the trailer not long before her death. At the moment of climax there was a flash of light. Rose explained it away as heat lightning, Warren shining a flashlight, or a car turning around in the yard. At the time Albro wondered if it could be Archie spying on Rose or Warren taking a photograph of Albro and Rose. When Albro's wife comes to his workshop to tell him about the murders, she sees the bench littered with empty vanilla bottles, guesses at the affair, and warns Albro to keep quiet. "He knew that much, anyway" (187),

Albro thinks at the end of the story, but he harbors the fear that he could be Archie's next victim. As in earlier stories, the desire for revenge and the fear of it have become all-consuming emotions.

"Negatives"

The final story in the enlarged edition of *Heart Songs* is "Negatives," first published in the July 1994 issue of *Esquire*. Another story about outsiders' misperceptions of the rural poor, "Negatives" speaks to another of Proulx's ongoing interests: the various meanings of photographs and—by extension—of her own art.

In "Negatives" Walter Welter, a photographer, moves in with his wealthy lover, Buck B., who has been forced to retire from his job as the host of a television children's show. Drawn to northern New England by the scenery, he has built a huge glass house on a mountainside and taken up pottery.

Walter soon becomes obsessed with Albina Muth, a dirty, undernourished young woman whom Buck characterizes as one of "The Rural Downtrodden" (192). Walter regales Buck's dinner guests with fanciful stories about Albina—all of which are the products of his warped imagination. By October Albina has left her abusive husband or lover and her three children. Much to Buck's disgust, she has started sleeping in his Mercedes, "ruining" it, he claims, with the smell she leaves behind.

After she has begged him for weeks to take her picture, Walter photographs Albina naked in an old abandoned building that was once a poorhouse, posing her in increasingly degrading positions that portray her as a victim and betray his eroticized hostility toward her. When he orders her to squat above "a mound of broken glass, splinters and curved blades sloped in a truncated cone," he experiences a "hot feeling" and knows the photograph will "be a tremendous image" (200). After he photographs her crawling into the oven of an old stove, she finally objects, saying she wants the photographs to show her as cute or "maybe like sexy" (201). He persuades her to stand on the stove for one more photograph. When she falls through the rusted metal of the water reservoir and stands there with bleeding feet—looking "as though she were to be immolated in some terrible rite" (201)—Walter, instead of helping her, laughs at her and subjects her to brutal sex. Later he pays her forty dollars and tells her not to sleep in Buck's Mercedes anymore.

At home Walter develops his film, convinced that the photographs will be an artistic success. Buck, who has become increasingly distressed by Walter's obsession with Albina, tells Walter to take the "ruined" Mercedes and leave. Buck has decided to sell the house anyway. All the bulldozing of trees to build more expensive houses like his has destroyed his view. (He can now see the old poorhouse with binoculars.) Walter takes his negatives and drives away in his "consolation prize," thinking that he can "have the interior steam-cleaned or deodorized or something" (203). Like Snipe in "Heart Songs," Buck and Walter both have the means to go elsewhere when situations do not meet their expectations. Buck's dream of enjoying the scenery has not included the poor people who live there or the influx of wealthy people like him whose building projects despoil the natural beauty of the region without appreciably helping its people. Walter, whose taste for the "down and dirty" is not unlike Snipe's, has no real concern for the people either. His interest in Albina is as the object of his fantasies, not as a human being to be understood or helped. Now that he has his negatives, her fate no longer concerns him.

In "Negatives" Proulx sketches characters who approach grotesque caricatures. Their names provide essential clues about their psyches. Buck B. has a name that is both tough sounding and cute. It is appropriate for someone who seems essentially asexual and comically naive in his desire to avoid anything disturbing in art or life; yet, as a wealthy man, he exerts power over others and harms them by his indifference. Buck's friend Barb Cigar is more dangerous, and more masculine, than Buck. Walter Welter's name suggests his underlying sadism, while Albina Muth is the white moth drawn to Walter's destructive flame for immolation.

Proulx's treatment of Walter and his photographs shows her realization of the danger inherent in his art. Walter's photographs are expressions of his vision, not representations of reality. They are "choked down and spare, out-of-focus, the horizons tilted, unrecognizable objects looming in the foreground, the heads of people quartered and halved" (194). His best photograph, he thinks, is one of a small house with an arbor: "Guests sorting through the photographs kept coming back to this dull scene until gradually the image of the house showed its secret hostility, the arbor turned harsh and offensive, the heavy grass bent with rage. The strength of the photograph emerged as though the viewer's eye was itself a developing medium. It would have happened faster, said Buck, if Walter wrote out the caption: *The House where Ernest and Lora Cool were Bludgeoned by their Son, Buxton Cool.*" Buck is not interested in Walter's explanation: "If you have to say what something's about, . . . it's not about anything except you saying it's about something" (194). Buck and his friends want Walter to take nature photographs, to create beautiful pictures that do not disturb their carefully created serenity. Barb Cigar, wants Walter to photograph the "lovely perfect leaves" (193) on her trees.

In "Dead Stuff," an article published in *Aperture* (Fall 1997) and later excerpted in *Harper's* (April 1998), Proulx wrote about the increase in interest during the 1980s and 1990s in photographic "images of death and the grotesque."[3] Buck and Barb's taste in photography dates to an earlier, and still popular, aesthetic that expects the photographer to create objective portraits of pleasing subjects without the intrusion of a personal perspective. Like his photographer friends—who send him prints of "an arrangement of goat intestines on backlit glass, a dead wallaby in a waterhole, a man . . . swallowing a squid tentacle coming out of a burning escalator" (194)—Walter's photographs are clearly of the new school, not just in their choice of subject but in their manipulation of their images to convey a particular meaning.

Though she too manipulates her subjects, Proulx has no sympathy for Walter's method, particularly in his photographing of Albina. The difference between her technique and Walter's may be inferred from a statement she makes in praise of Andrea Modica's photographs of people in Delaware County, New York, who are living in rural poverty like that described in Proulx's fiction. Modica, Proulx writes in "Reliquary" (1996), "entered into an intimacy with the situation of the place,"[4] Unlike Walter, who remains outside his subjects and uses them for personal objectives, Modica immerses herself in the culture that she shapes into art.

In another statement in "Reliquary" Proulx examines the question of objectivity. Discussing why Modica calls her prints "reliquaries," Proulx writes: "Whose relics? For the young girl who is the central focus of these photographs, they may serve as relics of a childhood; for Modica they may represent fragments of a place, people and time in her eye's life; for the viewer the images may fall into an interior reliquary of secret personal experiences and memories."[5] Proulx touches on a similar diversity of meanings in "Electric Arrows," when the narrator's aunt refuses to sell Mrs. Moon-Azure the Clews' family photographs, which were taken by the talented hired man whose house the Clews now inhabit. As the narrator explains, "What Aunt is afraid of is that the Moon-Azures will pass the pictures around among their weekend guests, that they will find their way into books and newspapers, we will someday see our grandfather's corpse in his homemade coffin resting on two sawhorses, flattened out on the pages of some magazine and labeled with a cruel caption" (164).

In "Negatives" one of Walter's friends has found an Inuit cache of old negatives. Mostly uninteresting snapshots of missionaries, they also include a photograph of a dead Inuit child. Like the Clews' picture of their dead grandfather, it is the sort of memorial photograph that was popular in earlier times. When Buck asks Walter what this photograph means, Walter explains, "It only meant something to the one who put this negative in the tobacco can" (195). As Proulx has explained, "Above all memorial photographs were personal, produced for a specific bereaved family, showing a specific individual, and often displaying anecdotal content."[6] One of the German families in *Accordion Crimes* (1996) also has a memorial photograph of a child, taken after tying his small corpse to a chair to keep him upright. These photographs, as well as the Clews' other treasured photographs, have a meaning to their owners that no one unacquainted with their subjects could begin to comprehend. They, like Modica's images, are the work of a sympathetic and gifted photographer, but the Clews' photographs are a different kind of art from Modica's, or Proulx's, because their creator has not expressed his vision of life through them. Unlike Walter's photograph of the Cools' house, they do need captions. Outside the context for which they were made, their meaning is imposed on them by the viewer, who draws from a separate "reliquary" of personal experiences and prejudices to create what may indeed be a "cruel caption."

Proulx's fiction occupies a place between Walter's cruel, essentially narcissistic images and the hired man's affectionate but self-effacing photographs. She establishes an intimacy with her characters and settings and treats her subjects without cruelty even when she gives them horrific fates to convey her vision of greater truths.

CHAPTER THREE

Postcards

The Second World War was the catalyst for a series of major changes in American life. The trend toward urbanization that had begun earlier in the twentieth century accelerated during the war as large numbers of people left rural areas to serve in the military or work in the defense industry. Few of them returned to their rural homes after the war. In the 1950s big corporations, chain stores, and large-scale agribusiness began to drive locally owned stores and small farms into economic ruin as one national market replaced smaller, regional markets. The people left behind in these major social changes are the subject of Proulx's first novel, *Postcards* (1992), which chronicles the slow decline of a Vermont family and their farm from 1944 until 1988. In the process the novel examines the significance of the American experience in the second half of the twentieth century.

In its ambitious scope the novel has much in common with John Dos Passos's *U.S.A.* trilogy (1930–1936), which attempts to do the same for the first three decades of the century. Proulx's novel also has stylistic similarities to Dos Passos's work. Proulx's "post-cards," which introduce all but one of the chapters, function like Dos Passos's "newsreel" sections in keeping the reader oriented in time and place. Proulx's postcards also help the reader fill in gaps between chapters: "The reader writes most of the story," she told an interviewer in 1992.[1] In addition, *Postcards* has chapters called "What I See," which present the immediate perceptions of one of the characters—usually those of the protagonist, Loyal Blood—and function in much the same way as "The Camera Eye" sections of Dos Passos's trilogy.

Proulx has said that her novel was inspired by some Vermont fire marshal's reports from the 1930s that included "a number of dismal accounts of farmers burning down their houses and barns for the meager insurance money." Proulx also made use of historical research in creating Loyal Blood, the handsome protagonist of *Postcards,* who "leaped complete and whole formed from a 1930s Vermont state prison mug shot" on one of "a small stack of postcards sent out by the Windsor Prison warden's office in the 1930s to alert various sheriffs around the state to escapees."[2] In the autumn of 1944, tall, strong, wavy-haired Loyal is the only hope for the survival of his family's farm, which has declined since the time when his grandfather kept trotting horses and merino sheep. Having studied agriculture, agronomy, and dairy management, Loyal has plans to reclaim pastures from the gradually encroaching woods and establish a profitable commercial dairy farm.

Yet all Loyal's plans are destroyed by his quick temper, which has been passed down from grandfather to father to son through merciless beatings for minor offenses. Their anger disappears as fast as it appears, leaving them "mild as milk afterwards," according to Loyal's mother, Jewell.[3] The novel opens at the dramatic moment when Loyal realizes that he has killed his fiancée, Billy, in the act of raping her. He decides he must run away: "Even before he got up he knew he was on his way" (1). Loyal's ultimate act of destruction is the catalyst for all the events that follow, spelling disaster not only for him but also for his family. Denying "his natural calling as a farmer," Loyal embarks on a journey that Proulx has called "an ironic and miniature version of the American frontier expansion westward."[4]

As Loyal hides Billy's body in an abandoned fox den built in a stone wall on the farm, he thinks that "it wasn't his fault but they'd say it was" (4). As the novel progresses, it becomes apparent that this refusal to accept responsibility for his anger and its consequences, whatever the complex underlying roots, is the result of Loyal's belief that his rage is somehow outside himself and his understanding. This denial of the guilt he recognizes in his heart—as much or even more than his crime—condemns Loyal to a life of endless wandering. He is running away from himself.

Loyal tells his family that he and Billy are leaving right away to go to the West together, that she has decided not even to say good-bye to her family. His departure sparks an episode of rage in his father, Minkton (appropriately nicknamed Mink, after a small member of the weasel family almost as well known for its quick temper as its valuable pelt). Destroying all the possessions Loyal has left behind, Mink even kills the Holstein cows that Loyal has persuaded him to buy and drags their bodies into the swamp for the wild animals to eat. These actions prompt Jewell to think that Mink's anger is "so wasteful he would have to burn for it in a hell as crimson as the landscape seen through the red cellophane strip on cigarette packs" (16). The wastefulness of anger is a major theme in *Postcards* as Proulx examines its effects on enraged people and the subjects of their rage.

For Loyal sex and death are inextricably entwined with his anger and often-denied guilt. While he is killing Billy, he experiences asthma-like symptoms. Twice later—on his first stop after leaving home and a few months later in Chicago on New Year's Eve—sexual arousal triggers the same symptoms, more severe each time. In Chicago a doctor who happens to be nearby saves Loyal's life by giving him a shot of Adrenalin. The doctor surmises that Loyal has had an allergic reaction to something he ate or drank, but Loyal knows otherwise: "It was the touching. Touching the woman. If it wasn't Billy it wouldn't be anyone else. The price for getting away. No wife, no family, no children, no human comfort on the quotidian unfolding of his life; for him, restless shifting from one town to another, the narrow fences of solitary thought, the pitiful easement of masturbation, lopsided ideas and soliloquies so easily transmuted to crazy mouthings. . . . some kind of black mucky channel that ran from his genitals to his soul had begun to erode" (53). The significance of Loyal's name now becomes clear. He will be faithful to Billy not through any conscious choice but in his "blood." His loyalty has been created by his unconscious mind and is enforced by his body.

Earlier as he drove away from the farm, he reflected on the irony of his situation. Billy, who had wanted to leave, is staying while Loyal, "who'd never thought beyond the farm, never wanted anything but the farm was on his way" (12). Later in the novel Loyal's memories of Billy fill in some of the events that led up to her murder. Sexy, red-haired Billy, who wanted to leave Vermont and had ambitions for a singing career, refused to have sexual relations with Loyal for fear of getting pregnant: "I'm not going to end up on your goddamn farm pouring slops to the pigs and looking a hundred years old before I'm forty with a big belly every year and kids all over the place" (73). She was convinced they could make a lot on money someplace other than Vermont. Two people so different in every way seem ill-suited, but Loyal found himself wanting only her. On the night of her murder he took her to the top of a hill to look down on the accomplishment of which he was proudest: a field he spent four or five years turning into "the best pasture in the county." To Billy, however, it was a "stupid old field" (13). In a flash of anger he took by force what she had denied him, killing her in the process. As a result, she is bound to the land he loves, and he is headed west on the journey she dreamed of taking with him.

At a tourist stop in the Adirondacks, where he tries unsuccessfully to have sex with the female proprietor and experiences the first of his post-Billy attacks, Loyal steals some seventy or eighty postcards, all with a photograph of a bear on the front. For more than forty years these cards are his only form of communication with his family, to whom he never gives a return address. He spends the winter of 1944–45 in Chicago, working in an aircraft factory and saving six hundred dollars with which he hopes to buy a small farm. While driving through Minnesota that spring, however, he gives a ride to two hitchhikers, the first of whom picks Loyal's pocket and takes off with most of the money. In an episode of magical realism the second man, an Indian called Blue Skies, conjures up a tornado to help him steal Loyal's car and the one hundred dollars hidden in Loyal's shoe, its location revealed by the gullible Loyal. Loyal is found scalped by the side of the road, without his shoes and socks and with only a notebook that Blue Skies has left behind. A postcard in the 1980s section of the novel lists the "1945 Tornado Car found in a Tree" as one of the tourist attractions in Cicero, South Dakota, and an obituary for a revered medicine man named Joe Blue Skies, sent on a postcard to a Rapid City, South Dakota, newspaper in 1988, says that he was blinded by injuries sustained in a tornado as a young man. Yet Proulx does not allow the reader to rest easy with this rational interpretation of events. She offers another possible identity for Blue Skies. In the late 1970s in Streaky Bacon, Montana, while looking through some old, discarded photographs of patients in a Fargo, North Dakota, mental hospital, Loyal finds a picture of a man he thinks is the Indian who robbed him. This man is identified as Walter Hairy Chin. This photograph—and by extension the photo-postcards that inspired Proulx's novel—has one meaning for the person who took it and yet another for the stranger who views it later. For Loyal and for the reader it offers no explanations, rational or otherwise, for the tornado of 1945. Was the Blue Skies who robbed and scalped Loyal a powerful medicine man capable of conjuring up a tornado, or was he a mad man who happened to be in Loyal's car when disaster struck?

By 1951 Loyal is working in a gold mine in Colorado. After he nearly dies in a cave-in, he decides to find an above-ground occupation and takes up uranium prospecting just as the prices for the ore are dropping and the day of the individual "rock rat" with a Geiger counter is passing. Then as prices start to rise again, big businesses take over, using expensive equipment and polluting the environment with "acid leaching, chemical extraction, . . . poison wastes and tailings, sand slurry choking the streams, big fish kills and mountains of dead and reeking tailings" (147). The novel is full of examples of how Americans have been poor stewards of the land, gradually losing any sense of connection to the natural world and the creatures that inhabit it.

While searching for uranium, Loyal begins finding fossilized dinosaur bones and selling them to "Donald the Bone Man," who has connections to museums and universities. Searching for hidden bones is an oddly fitting occupation for a man who has a hidden skeleton in his past, and Loyal is especially good at it. By 1963 he has been hired by an experienced dinosaur hunter, who marvels at Loyal's skills. Earlier in the novel, Loyal's younger brother, Dub, described Loyal's painstaking methods of trapping foxes. Loyal uses the same talents for hunting bones. He works by "part instinct for the way animals might move through a country, part feeling for the millennial landscape, an interior knowledge that suggested where lakes and mud wallows, where sinkholes and fissures had been in the vanished world" (157).

In the summer of 1965 Loyal teams up with a young graduate student who shares his interest in the tracks of the duckbill platypus, which suggest that scientists have been wrong about the creature's anatomy. The two plan to work together the following summer, but the student chokes to death on his own vomit after using drugs at a party, leaving Loyal wondering why things always seem to turn out wrong for him and thinking that his plans with the student were the "closest he'd ever coming to doing something of value" (167).

By the fall of 1966 Loyal has given up dinosaur hunting and gone to help Ben Rainwater, a wealthy, eccentric, self-confessed alcoholic, build an observatory on his ranch in New Mexico. Ben tells Loyal that humankind has lost any sense of connection to the sky: "Most of the world sees nothing above but the sun, conveniently situated to give them cancerous tans and good golf days" (171).

Ben's intuitive grasp of astronomy parallels Loyal's ingrained knowledge of the land, and it is fitting that Ben senses Loyal's deep-seated emotional conflict. The usually taciturn Loyal describes the reaction he has when he is sexually aroused by women, attributing it to "something that happened long ago. Something I did" (172), but

when Ben suggests psychiatric help, Loyal refuses, saying, "Life crip-
ples us up in different ways but it gets everybody. It gets everybody is
how I look at it. Gets you again and again and one day it wins" (173).

This sense of fatalism is typical of Loyal, as well as of many
other characters in the novel. For much of his long journey he writes
in his "Indian's books," the first of which is the notebook left behind
by the Indian who robbed him in Minnesota. Whenever he tries to
write about what happened the night he killed Billy, he fails. He
lacks the self-knowledge necessary to explain his act and is afraid to
seek it. His fatalism is symptomatic of his unwillingness to examine
his actions and their underlying causes.

In 1968, when he is fifty-one, Loyal takes stock of his life and
decides that he may yet have time to settle down on a farm and work
on curing his "trouble with earth" (187). Using the money he has
saved for years, he buys a farm in North Dakota. Though he half
believes that the farm work might rid him of his anger and guilt, a
disturbing dream in which Ben metamorphoses into a woman convinces Loyal that his affliction is not cured. As he awakes to find his
body covered with large red weals, he realizes that he "still had his
anger, hot as new blood. And hated it in himself" (189). Instead of
the wife and children for whom he longs, he settles for a puppy to
which he gives the ironic name Little Girl.

Not all Loyal's knowledge of farming in Vermont can be
applied to farming in North Dakota. In fact two of his "improve-
ments" are indirectly responsible for his next round of "bad luck."
In October 1969, after a dry summer, wind-blown tumbleweed balls
pile up around Loyal's house as high as the second-story windows
and are held in place by Loyal's new fence and windbreak. Then the
manager at the new McDonald's, an ignorant easterner, attempts to

clear the tumbleweed from his parking lot by pouring gasoline on it and setting it on fire. The result is a conflagration that sweeps across the countryside, destroying sixteen farms, including Loyal's, on which he has no fire insurance. The fire objectifies his submerged anger, which flares up and destroys what he loves because he has never learned to control it.

Left only with his dog and his truck, Loyal sells his land and takes up trapping, building a primitive house trailer that he pulls behind his truck. During the 1970s he traps coyote, getting top prices for his beautifully cured pelts. By the end of the decade, however, animal-rights activists have driven down the demand for fur, depriving trappers of their livelihood.

Loyal traps for several seasons on the ranch of Jack and Starr Sagine, the first couple with whom he develops a friendship. Now nearly sixty, Loyal discovers he can be near Starr and even have sexual fantasies about her without experiencing his old symptoms. Yet, after Jack dies in 1979 and Starr hints that Loyal could settle on the ranch as her lover, Loyal is afraid to risk intimacy with her and leaves the next morning, cutting off yet another road to human companionship.

Throughout the novel the red-haired Billy is associated with red foxes and coyotes. At about the time Loyal decides to give up trapping, he finds a young female red coyote in one of his traps. As she looks at him with "her body language, mingling appeasement, fear, anger, threat, resignation, pain, horror, and more, the terrible and thrilling sense of her life's imminent end" (267), Loyal is reminded of Billy. Aware that she is not too injured to survive on her own, Loyal releases her in a symbolic act of atonement, giving her the freedom to live the life that he once denied Billy. (Earlier the faithful and much-loved Little Girl has been accidentally killed in one of Loyal's traps, creating an ironic parallel to Billy's fate.)

By 1982 Loyal is suffering from a symbolically appropriate chronic lung ailment. He has become a collector of hats and old cowboy-movie memorabilia, pathetically clinging to other people's memories because he has so few good ones of his own. Once taciturn, he now talks endlessly, trying to make human connections wherever he can, but the people he tells about his various adventures tend not to believe his stories. Soon his trailer and the entire uninsured collection are stolen, leaving him more homeless and uprooted than ever. He drifts into the "Stream of migrant labor," and, as Proulx writes, "It's easier to get into the Stream than out again" (279).

In 1984 Loyal takes a job as foreman of a gang of potato pickers. Alerted by the ceaseless cawing of the crows in a nearby cottonwood grove, he discovers that the owner of the farm has been killing migrant workers and burying them there so that he does not have to pay them. Loyal sends the sheriff an anonymous postcard and leaves town quickly.

The bodies Loyal finds in the cottonwood grove create an eerie parallel to his own crime, and the connection is heightened by something else he finds there. At first he thinks it is the largest and most valuable dinosaur bone he has ever seen, but a scientist in Rapid City, South Dakota, explains that Loyal's find is a fulgurite, formed when lightning struck the ground. The fulgurite is indeed valuable. Now sixty-seven, ill and disoriented, Loyal decides to take the fulgurite to a man who used to buy dinosaur bones from him during the 1960s. He thinks the man was in Utah or Montana, but he was actually in Wyoming. Sure that he will recognize the place when he sees it, Loyal sets out in the wrong direction and ends up in Minnesota, where his ancient truck breaks down. He buries the fulgurite thinking he can find it later and sets out on foot with only the possessions he can carry on his back.

By the manner in which it was created and the way in which he hides it, the fulgurite suggests Loyal's crime and the guilt he has carried with him ever since. Yet it also represents Loyal's whole life, which was shaped by his father's flashes of anger just as the fulgurite was formed by lightning. Loyal has had many talents, but he has squandered them in his ceaseless flight from facing his demons. His crime has wasted not only Billy's life but his own and his family's as well.

Early in the book Proulx includes a "biography" of the bear whose picture is on the postcards that Loyal sends his family. As the book progresses, it becomes apparent that Loyal is like that bear. When the bear was four, a shotgun blast of broken screws left it mentally unstable, much as Mink's beatings have predisposed Loyal to resort to violence. The bear was photographed while scavaging in the garbage heap at a lodge in the Adirondacks, where the owner had set up benches so that his guests at the lodge could watch the bear and laugh at it. The bear, which was "insensitive to the subtle implications of new things" (33), was accidentally electrocuted after electricity was run to the lodge in 1926. Loyal may also be described as "insensitive to the subtle implications of new things," and during his last lonely journey on foot, he is seen scavenging for food in a garbage dumpster outside a Minneapolis restaurant. Never having held a job in which he contributed to the Social Security system, he has lived off the land by old ways at a time when modern society has become increasingly divorced from the land and traditional ways of life. While he was trapping coyotes during the 1970s Loyal learned about a huge illegal poaching scheme in which black bears were being killed for their gall bladders, which were sold as aphrodisiacs in the Far East. One of the federal wildlife agents who broke up the ring predicted to Loyal, "We are going to see the end of the bears in our lifetime" (258). Loyal and his way of life are becoming as anachronistic as the bear.

Shortly before he searches for food in the dumpster, a lost and disoriented Loyal wanders into a meadow and begins dancing with a rotting branch. When he stumbles, he exclaims: "'Trip me, you bitch. Get out.' Panting, retching with the cough. And hurled the branch, glad to see it break in a spray of red pulp. His loneliness was not innocent" (300). Loyal's anger has consumed him, making him a grotesque, scarcely human, creature. His shambling, bearlike outward demeanor mirrors his inner deformity. Appropriately enough, the bear and weasel families were traditionally considered to be related. Loyal is truly his father's son.

As Loyal lies dying, he has a vision in which the Indian's book opens and the pages become the field on the Vermont farm with the wall where he buried Billy at the top. In death he has returned home. One of the ironies of the novel, however, is that he could probably have gone home and resumed his life on the farm within a year or two of leaving. No one ever questions his story about going away with Billy, and in April 1945, when his postcard home informs his family that Billy has left him for another man, neither they nor Billy's relatives doubt his word. The only other living being who knows Billy's whereabouts is the family dog, which was with Loyal when he killed her. Yet in January 1945, when the dog brings one of Billy's shoes to Loyal's younger sister, Mernelle, she fails to understand its significance, uses it to play a game of fetch with the dog, and finally tosses it on the roof of the milk house. Years later, in 1977, Franklin Witkin, the Boston doctor who has bought the land where the wall still stands, finds Billy's body while removing stones from the wall to build a patio. With his tendency to romanticize the past (like the Moon-Azures in "Electric Arrows") Witkin decides that he has found the grave of an "early settler's wife, exhausted by childbearing, or, perhaps, scalped and slain by Indians, or killed by typhoid or pneumonia or milk fever" (255). Deciding not to "desecrate" her grave, he restores her resting place without ever noticing the sole of her other shoe, which presumably would have revealed that her burial was far more recent than he thinks. The demons pursuing Loyal are of his own making.

Though Loyal's story is central to the novel, *Postcards* devotes equal time to the fate of the family and the farm Loyal has left behind. Without Loyal's help his father and younger brother, Marvin (known as Dub), cannot handle the farm work. Known even to himself as "the fool of the family" (7), Dub is a wanderer by nature, a lover of popular music and dancing, and as his name suggests, an improviser rather than a planner. Having lost an arm in an accident while riding the rails, he can do no more than carry milk buckets for his father, who becomes saddled with the task of doing all the milking. Even after cutting the size of the herd, they cannot cope on their own, and the farm goes rapidly downhill.

By December 1951 the Bloods are down to nine cows—all suffering from Mad Itch. Dub's wife has left him, taking his only child, because he cannot support them while working on the family farm, and he has been unable to find another job. Dub blames the breakup of his marriage partly on his father's stubborn refusal to allow agricultural experts to visit the farm and advise them and partly on their failure to get electricity, which despite wartime promises has been installed in towns first and has not yet made it to some rural areas. Mink's brother, Ott (short for Otter), has sold his old farm and bought one that has electricity. He has listened to the experts and established a prosperous dairy farm like the one Loyal dreamed of.

Mink's perception of his situation points to an even more fundamental change: "Poorer every year, the work harder, the prices higher, the chances of pulling out of it fewer and fewer." He is used to being poor; his family and all their neighbors have always been poor, but when he was young, "things kept going, like a waterwheel turning under the weight of flowing water. Relatives and neighbors came without asking to fill in. Where the hell were they now when he was sinking under black water?" (103). Now most of his longtime neighbors and his extended family are gone. Though their fate might have been different if Loyal had remained, the Bloods are victims of larger economic trends over which they have little control. The failures of small family farms unable to compete with modern agribusiness have also caused the decline of traditional support networks as more and more people leave rural areas in search of work.

Convinced that the farm is worthless, that they would not be able to break even if they sold it, Mink tells Dub to burn down the barn for the insurance money. The company pays their claim of $2,000, but then an ambitious young investigator becomes suspicious. Mink and Dub are convicted of arson and sent to prison. The insurance company demands repayment of the money.

In prison Mink's anger turns inward, and within months he has hanged himself in his cell. In despair Jewell sends a postcard to Loyal care of general delivery at his last known location, but he has moved on, and this message, like other efforts to communicate with him, never reaches him. Unable to run the farm with only Mernelle's help and needing to repay the insurance company, Jewell sells Loyal's field to Ott and the woodlot above the field to Witkin, who wants to build a hunting camp. She is left with the house, a yard big enough for a garden, and after all the debts are paid, eight hundred dollars.

Otters, like minks, are members of the weasel family and prized for their fur. Like minks, they can be fierce fighters. Yet, unlike their relatives, they are playful, sociable animals, and Ott lives up to his name. In contrast to his isolated brother, who saw a breakdown of the old ways but did not understand the social and economic changes that replaced them, Ott has learned the true value of real estate in the new order. The baby boom and the urban prosperity that followed the Second World War have created a different market for land, not for farming, but for housing and vacation retreats. Ott makes a sizable profit from Loyal's field by dividing it into forty half-acre lots—which remind Jewell of cemetery plots—and creating a mobile-home park. Jewell also discovers that his partner in this venture is Ronnie Nipple, once Loyal's best friend and the real-estate agent who found the buyers for her land at what he claimed was the best possible price.

By 1969 Ott's trailer park is polluting Loyal's field and the surrounding area with sewage and noise. This gross indignity inflicted on the land that Loyal so lovingly husbanded to its full potential repeats on a small scale the despoiling of the environment that he sees on his travels around the country, underlining how postwar entrepreneurs have become poor stewards of a land from which they have become emotionally and intellectually divorced. This divorce parallels those between humans in the novel, another kind of failure to connect.

Dub becomes one of the postwar entrepreneurs, his prosthetic arm of "lifelike" plastic symbolizing his lack of feeling for nature. In November 1953, newly released from prison and having informed Jewell by postcard that he is not returning to the farm, he goes to Florida, where he drifts into the real-estate business for lack of any other ambition except the desire to be rich. He has already made his mark in commercial real estate by 1967, when he marries Pala, a young woman he recognized at first meeting as "a pirate" (184). Together they make millions in land deals, in part through secret negotiations to develop a large track of untouched swamp land into Disney World. Aware that the project is ecologically unwise and that it will replace native species of fauna and flora with "[e]xpensive plastic shit," he nonetheless "winks and says to himself, thanks a million" (203). Their wealth diminished by a tax audit in 1979 and their love of Florida shaken by the Miami riots of 1984, Dub and Pala continue to thrive. Pala decides they should go to Houston, where she can start a travel agency while Dub, who has retired, can continue his hobby of growing orchids. Marking Dub's first attempt at any sort of horticulture, this avocation is well suited to a man with no sense of connection to the land, for orchids live without contact to the soil.

Mernelle, who shares Dub's lack of interest in farming, survives her traumatic, poverty-stricken teenage years and marries Ray MacWay, who rises from equal economic depths to make a decent living for them in the lumber business. Mernelle becomes a typical 1950s-style middle-class housewife, more like the women she sees on television than her mother. Mernelle's only regret is her inability to bear children, which is echoed by the sterility of her lifestyle.

As her name suggests, Jewell Blood is a valuable part of her family. She is the repository of the old values and her family's history, and after Mink's death she proves able to bridge the old and the new. Faced with the necessity of making her own way, she learns to drive and takes a job at the local cannery, where she likes the work and the companionship of the other women. She also knits garments for two women who own a chain of ski shops. She is amused by their idea of the "country" look—neutral colors and rough-textured yarn that is far below the quality of the yarn women of her generation and those before them used to spin at home with wool from their own sheep.

In the mid-1960s, after the farmhouse starts to fall down and she moves into a new trailer on her land, she continues to keep up her gardens behind the old house, even as the woodchucks and deer, now safe from the traps that Loyal used to put out, threaten to take it over. Having discovered that boys do not go in for trapping as they once did, she is nonetheless determined to keep her little patch of land from going "wild again," exclaiming, "I worked on getting them gardens up the way I like for most of my grown-up life and I am not about to turn them over to the wildlife" (174). Though Ray and Mernelle have given her a freezer, she goes back to canning her vegetables, because she does not like the way the frozen ones tasted in March "when they were full of ice crystals" (175). She also complains about the lack of flavor in store-bought meat, remembering the taste of fresh-killed chicken, and she praises the superior taste and texture of home-canned beef and deer meat over frozen.

Jewell's love of the land and her appreciation of the old ways are
the legacy that she has passed on to Loyal, but after Mink's death frees
her from the drudgery of a farm wife's life and the domination of a
quick-tempered husband, she begins to exhibit traits like Dub's as
well. Living in her trailer, where she has electricity and indoor plumbing for the first time in her life, she appreciates many of the conve-
niences of modern life. Certainly Proulx does not suggest that Jewell
is wrong to do so. Unlike Dub, Jewell keeps the old and new in balance, rather than wholeheartedly embracing modernity like her son
and discarding tradition and all concern for the natural environment.

One trait that Jewell shares with Dub, however, becomes her
eventual downfall: wanderlust. Once she learns to drive, Jewell
develops a newfound sense of freedom and begins to understand the
appeal of the "views" outsiders praise. Men, she decides, do not
understand women's lives, "the profound sameness, week after
week, after month of the same narrow rooms . . . . You couldn't get
away from your troubles." Moreover, she decides, men "seemed to
believe, as in a religion that women were numbed by an instinctive
craving to the wet mouths of babies, predestined to choose always
the petty points of life on which to hang their attention until at last
all ended and began with the orifices of the body. She had believed
it herself" (127).

As Jewell recognizes, her driving is an expression of her freedom from Mink's anger: "He had crushed her into a corner of life"
(127). By November 1969, when she is seventy-two, however, Jewell's driving and her judgment are becoming erratic. She decides one
cloudy morning to take a trip she has been longing to make and sets
out for Mount Washington in New Hampshire to drive up the toll
road and admire the views, overlooking the fact that the vistas she

expects to see from that mountaintop will be obscured by clouds. As she drives, rain turns to sleet. Rather than turning back, she attempts to take a shortcut down a logging road, where her Volkswagen Beetle gets hung up on a rock. While looking for a branch to use as a lever, she suffers a fatal aneurism in a gully full of brambles. Her body is never found.

The results of Jewell's final "pilgrimage" suggest that her downfall is at least partially the result of her seduction by a modern way of life that she only partially understands. At the same time, however, the inability of a full-scale search team to find her body is a positive outcome for a woman who has spent her final years enjoying her freedom. Mernelle finds Jewell's wedding ring, which Jewell took off after Mink's suicide, and buries it beside her father. Dub pays for an iron railing around the burial plot, but Jewell is not there. She remains free, wedded to the countryside she loves.

Jewell escapes the fate of her good friend Opaline Nipple, who devoted much of her life to pretending not to notice that her husband, appropriately nicknamed Toot, was a drinker and womanizer. After surgery for prostate cancer left him impotent, he hanged himself. Mrs. Nipple's approach to dealing with misfortune is to keep a spotless house and pretend that nothing is wrong. She comes to a comic-ironic end when she falls through the rotting floor boards near her kitchen pump, refuses medical treatment, and contracts tetanus from being punctured by rusty nails. "When I think how all that rot was layin' there under that proud housekeeping," comments Jewell. "There's a lesson in it" (69). Mrs. Nipple's household is a metaphor for her family, fine on the surface but rotten beneath, like Ronnie who used his friendship with Loyal to take advantage of Jewell.

When she falls through the floor, Mrs. Nipple lands on her daughter's baby, a toddler who has been the subject of an extensive search by most of the neighborhood. As when he brought Mernelle one of Billy's shoes, the Bloods' dog knows where the baby is all along, but when he sticks his nose under the porch steps and sniffs, he seems so comical that no one pays any attention to him.

The novel includes several comic set pieces, most notably the scene in the insurance office at the time the investigator decides to investigate the Bloods' barn fire and Ray McWay's courtship of Mernelle, whom he met through a newspaper campaign to find him a wife. Proulx also creates humor at the expense of outsiders, especially Dr. Franklin Saul Witkin, the Boston dermatologist who buys the woodlot above Loyal's field. Witkin, whose name suggests "small wit" or "little sense," has had "fantasies of wilderness" (129) since childhood. He loves the woods but is unable to tell one tree from another and gets lost whenever he ventures into the woods alone. He romanticizes nature, feeling an "atavistic yearning" (165) in the woods, but he does not understand it.

Americans of the late twentieth century, Proulx implies, are far more likely to be like Witkin than like Loyal, with his deep understanding and respect for the land and its flora and fauna. The result is the exploitation and despoliation of nature by some of the same people who romanticize it, as well as traditional, rural ways of life. As the novel ends with Loyal's dying alone and away from home, the reader is left with a sense of loss, regretting the waste of a man's talents and the broad implications of his failure to pass on his knowledge and love of the land.

At the same time, however, the reader is haunted by the senselessness of Loyal's brutal crime and the intensity of his irrational anger. If, as Proulx says, his wanderings are "an ironic version of American expansion westward,"[5] then he is a deeply flawed representation of the American pioneer. His crime and his anger become symbols of the racial and ethic hatreds and the endemic violence that have plagued the United States throughout its history. *Postcards* is finally a microcosmic depiction of a deeply flawed nation, a subject that Proulx treats more openly and on a broader canvas in *Accordion Crimes.*

CHAPTER FOUR

The Shipping News

The Shipping News (1993), Proulx's widely acclaimed second novel, is her only full-length work of fiction with what might be called a hopeful ending. The enthusiastic reviewer for the *Washington Post Book World* went so far as to call the book "a wildly comic heart-thumping romance."[1] Other critics echoed that viewpoint. Yet for all the humor of the novel and its hero's discovery of contentment and self-worth, the so-called happy ending is qualified by an awareness that his definition of happiness is severely limited and by Proulx's warnings about the consequences of modern humanity's loss of community and attachment to the land.

Most of the novel is set in Newfoundland, which Proulx visited for the first time in the mid-1980s. As she wrote in 1997, she found the Great Northern Peninsula of the island to be "a place of deepest personal significance."[2] She became fascinated with the fishing families following hard, traditional lifestyles in that unforgiving climate, and immersed herself in studying their history, culture, lore, and language. One of her happiest discoveries during her research for *The Shipping News* was G. M. Story, W. J. Kirwin, and J. D. A. Widdowson's *Dictionary of Newfoundland English* (1982), which she calls "one of the major lexigraphical works of this century."[3] Yet, as in the rural New England she depicted in *Heart Songs* and *Postcards,* Proulx "could also see contemporary civilization rushing in on the island after its centuries of isolation," and in *The Shipping News* she once again placed her characters "against a background of

incomprehensible and massive social change" in which the economic basis for their traditional society is on the verge of collapse.[4]

Many of the chapters are named for different kinds of knots and
headed with sketches and descriptions of them, mostly from *The
Ashley Book of Knots,* an encyclopedic reference work first published in 1944. The epigraph to the novel also comes from that work
and suggests the complexity and the wide range of possibilities of
the human entanglements Proulx portrays in the book: "In a knot of
eight crossings there are 256 different 'over and under' arrangements possible. . . ."[5] Unlike the postcards in Proulx's first novel,
which fill in gaps in the story line, the sketches and headings in *The
Shipping News* serve the conventional function of providing the
reader with clues to the important themes of the chapters without
actually furthering the action of the novel. The heading for chapter
1, for example, explains the name of the protagonist, Quoyle, while
the one for chapter 2, "Love Knot," precedes his meeting with the
woman who becomes his first wife, an occasion on which "[a]n
invisible hand threw loops and crossings in Quoyle's intestines"
(12). Chapter 3, "Strangle Knot," describes how Quoyle is trapped
by his hopeless love for his undeserving wife. A few chapters later,
when Quoyle is in Newfoundland but has not yet established strong
ties there, the headnote describes a slippery hitch, which is especially useful when "the necessity . . . arises for instant casting off"
(71). The next chapter, however, in which Quoyle is beginning to
settle into his new way of life, is headed with a more secure knot—
the mooring hitch.

The headnote to chapter 1 explains that a quoyle is a "coil
of rope," and it goes on to define a particular kind of quoyle: "A

Flemish flake is a spiral coil of one layer only. It is made on deck, so that it may be walked on if necessary" (1). Thus, Quoyle is introduced as a kind of Everyman as loser. In his desperate need to be accepted and loved he allows people to take advantage of him. Tall, massively overweight, and with a huge "giant's chin," he is pathetically self-conscious, believing that his "chief failure, a failure of normal appearance," is the reason for his parents' clear preference for his brother (2). His lack of confidence seems to guarantee his failure at everything he tries. He embarks on each new venture with the conviction that he is incapable of succeeding and thus predisposes his every failure.

In keeping with his Everyman status, Quoyle's first name is never revealed. (Nearly three hundred pages into the novel, when he reaches what seems likely to be the highpoint of his professional career, his first and middle initials are revealed to be R. G., suggesting the dawning of his sense of individual self-worth.) While the names of other characters in the novel are sometimes suggestive, most are not as obviously meaningful as Quoyle's. For example, Billy Pretty seems never to have become sexually mature, while Tertius Card, whose first name is the Latin word for "third," is clearly a third-rate newsman. B. Beaufield Nutbeem, who plans to sail around the world in his "[m]odified Chinese junk" (94), is as eccentric as his name suggests, and Beety Buggit, an admirable character with a funny name, turns out to have a gift for stand-up comedy. The headnote to chapter 14, which introduces Quoyle's future wife, Wavey, suggests that her name is common in Newfoundland: "In Wyoming they name girls Skye. In Newfoundland it's Wavey" (122).

The novel begins with a survey of Quoyle's early life. Lacking the confidence to define and pursue goals, he drops out of college, eventually and accidentally ending up as a reporter for a small weekly "junk" newspaper in the aptly named upstate New York town of Mockingburg. Though Partridge, a friend and fellow journalist, teaches him some of the fundamentals of writing and organizing a story, Quoyle is a "third-rate newspaperman" (1), who

> abstracted his life from the times. He believed he was a newspaper reporter, yet read no paper except *The Mockingburg Record,* and so managed to ignore terrorism, climatological change, collapsing governments, chemical spills, plagues, recessions and failing banks, floating debris, the disintegrating ozone layer. Volcanoes, earthquakes and hurricanes, religious frauds, defective vehicles and scientific charlatans, mass murderers and serial killers, tidal waves of cancer, AIDS, deforestation and exploding aircraft were as remote to him as braid catches, canions and rosette-embroidered garters. (11)

(According the *Oxford English Dictionary,* canions are sausagelike rolls of fabric attached to the hems of breeches and were popular in the fifteenth and sixteenth centuries.)

Quoyle has "constructed an illusion of orderly progress" (11) by which to interpret his life. He spends much of the novel creating and struggling to maintain a series of illusions, some harmless, some ultimately destructive. Chief among them is the fiction that his wife, Petal Bear, loves him and their two daughters, Bunny and Sunshine. In fact, Petal Bear, who thinks she should have been named "Iron" or "Spike," tires of Quoyle soon after their marriage and, growing to hate "his cringing hesitancy," begins a series of sexual liaisons with every willing male she encounters. In another life, the narrator comments, Petal "would have been Genghis Khan," but, as a woman of the twentieth century, she expresses her aggression through "petty triumphs of sexual adventures" (13–14). Quoyle, who feels the "cables" of his love for Petal "tighten around him as though drawn up by a ratchet" (14), rationalizes her behavior. Even after her death, when Quoyle learns that she got money to run away with a lover by selling Bunny and Sunshine to a maker of pornographic movies, he insists that Petal was not a bad person, just "starved for love" (23). Her death in a car accident as she and her lover speed toward Florida only encourages Quoyle's invention of an imaginary loving Petal, for the children's sake as well as his own.

Petal's death and the rescue of the children before they have been sexually abused come soon after the joint suicide of his unloving parents, who have discovered they are dying of cancer. Quoyle is left with the funeral arrangements and the duty of contacting his father's sister, Agnis Hamm, who is to take charge of the father's ashes. Agnis convinces Quoyle, who has just lost his job and is floundering as usual, to go with her to their family's old home on the Great Northern Peninsula of Newfoundland, where he can start a new life for himself and his daughters. Though she wanted never to return there when she was a young woman, Agnis now confesses to "a longing to go back. Probably some atavistic drive to finish up where you started" (29).

Partridge finds Quoyle a job with a small weekly newspaper there, and, as the narrator has informed the reader on the first page, "At thirty-six, bereft, brimming with grief and thwarted love,

Quoyle steered away to Newfoundland, the rock that had generated his ancestors, a place he had never been nor thought to go" (1). In fact it is an unlikely destination for him. After all, the island is a "watery place. And Quoyle feared water, could not swim" (2)—a failure reinforced by his father's angry, repeated attempts to "teach" his son to do so by forcibly throwing him into various bodies of water.

Yet with its "six thousand miles of coast blind-wrapped in fog" (32), Newfoundland is also literally and figuratively a place apart from the modern world, a natural destination for a man who has managed to shut out so much reality from his conception of his life. Much later in the novel Billy Pretty explains how fog distorts reality: "It's an optical illusion, is the fog loom" (174).

The small town where Quoyle takes a job is named Killick-Claw, after one of the wooden "arms" of a "killick," which the *Dictionary of Newfoundland English* defines as a anchor made of a stone and pliable sticks used to moor small boats and fishing nets. The name is appropriate for the place where Quoyle establishes his moorings, but it is also ironic, because many of the residents are being forced by the decline in the fishing trade to move to the mainland in search of work.

Like small, rural towns everywhere, Killick-Claw seems turned in on itself, and its newspaper reveals its insularity. Clearly the work of amateurs, the *Gammy Bird* is the source of much humor in the novel. The headnote to chapter 7, "The Gammy Bird," explains that Newfoundlanders call the sociable common eider the "gammy bird." The name is derived from "gammying," a custom from the days of sail, "when two ships at sea would back their yards together and shout the news" (56).

The *Gammy Bird* is mainly a source of local news and gossip. B. Beaufield Nutbeem, who covers foreign news, gets his information from a static-ridden shortwave radio, "twisting the stories around to suit his mood of the day" (58). The stories are rewritten by Tertius (Tert) Card, the managing editor, whose laughable editing and typing skills create sentences "so richly freighted with typographical errors that the original authors would not recognize their own stories" (59). "Burmese sawmill owners and the Rangoon Development Corporation met in Tokyo Tuesday to consider a joint approach to marketing tropical hardwoods" becomes "Burnoosed sawbill awnings and the Ranger Development Competition met Wednesday near Tokyo to mark up topical hairwood" (59). Tert argues that Nutbeem's world news is "only stolen fiction in the first place," while Jack excuses Tert's typos because they "give humor to the paper" and are "better than a crossword puzzle" (59). Quoyle is surprised to see that the paper has "a staggering number of ads" (60), most of which, he learns later, are fabricated with the hope of impressing potential, paying advertisers.

The *Gammy Bird* also includes restaurant reviews praising food such as the fish-strip baskets that come with plastic packets of tartar sauce or lemon juice at "Grudge's Cod Hop" (61) and creating the impression that the provincial dish of Newfoundland may well be fried bologna. (Descriptions of home-cooked meals elsewhere in the novel suggest that Newfoundland does have some distinctive regional dishes—including moose meatballs and seal-flipper pie, which is actually made with shoulder meat.)

The founder and owner of the *Gammy Bird,* Jack Buggit, is a fisherman by training and inclination, but Canada has been "giving fishing rights to every country on earth" while "regulating us [New-

foundland fishermen] out of business" (65). After Canada Manpower made several misguided attempts to create jobs for him and
other Newfoundlanders, Jack—despite a lack of formal qualifica-
tions—persuaded the agency to give him the funds to start a weekly
newspaper.

Despite his professional inexperience, Jack has a true newspaperman's "genius" for the kind of stories his readers want. The center of reader interest in the *Gammy Bird* is "Scrunchions," a
"near-libelous" column of local gossip. (According to the *Dictionary of Newfoundland English,* "scrunchions" has several meanings,
including leftover food scraps, pieces of fat, and fried cubes of fat-
back pork used as garnishes.) Readers also like the three or four stories about sexual abuse that appear in every issue. The Englishman
Nutbeem, who covers this beat as well as foreign news, comments
later in the novel: "I've heard it said—cynically—that sexual abuse
of children is an old Newf tradition," only to have Tert reply that it
is "a Brit tradition" (218). Overlooking the implications of perversion at home, *Gammy Bird* readers particularly like stories that
"show the demented style of life in the States," demonstrating, Tert
explains, "the lunacy of those from away" (112). The paper also fea-
tures stories about automobile accidents, complete with photographs, in every issue, and the editorials spray "streams of
invective across the provincial political scene like a fire hose." The
Gammy Bird, Quoyle thinks, is "a hard bite. . . . A tough little paper"
(63). As Tert Card explains later, "every Newf paper does it now,
but *Gammy Bird* was first to give names and grisly details" (218).

Quoyle is sure that his previous journalistic experience has not
prepared him for this sort of reporting, and he becomes even more
certain about his inability to work for the paper when he gets his

assignments. In addition to the shipping news, which seems routine enough not to invoke Quoyle's fear of water, Jack tells him to cover car accidents, demanding a photograph of a wreck for the front page of every issue and explaining that, if there are no accidents in a given week, the paper has a large file of old wreck photographs that Quoyle can use.

Still traumatized by Petal's death in an automobile accident, Quoyle tells Agnis that he cannot do the job, but she responds that he is wrong, explaining, "We face up to awful things because we can't go around them, or forget them. The sooner you get it over with . . . the sooner you can get on with your own life." Quoyle thinks this advice is "[t]en-cent philosophy" (72), but Agnis seems not to be the only Newfoundlander with this point of view.

Later in the novel Nutbeem comments to Quoyle that Jack has an "uncanny sense about assignments." In fact, each reporter's beat is connected to his "private inner fears" (221). Not only is Quoyle covering car wrecks, but Nutbeem, who was sexually assaulted as a schoolboy, covers sexual-abuse cases, and Billy Pretty, a bachelor who has told Quoyle he has "a personal affliction" (171) that prevents him from being sexually attracted to women, covers home news and the women's page. Nutbeem is uncertain "if Jack understands what he's doing, if the pain is supposed to ease and dull through repetitive confrontation, or if it just persists," but by this time Quoyle realizes that Jack—who continues to go out fishing even though his father, grandfather, two brothers, and oldest son were all drowned—is doing "the same thing to himself." Quoyle is convinced that the repetition does dull the pain, "because you see your condition is not unique, that other people suffer as you suffer"

(221). In fact, Jack becomes a benevolent father figure to Quoyle, whose own father has offered him nothing but rejection.

The death of Petal is not the only part of Quoyle's past with which he must come to terms. He must also learn about and reach an understanding of his family's history in a place where, despite Agnis's yearnings for it, the Quoyles are the subjects of derision. Quoyle, says Agnis before they leave for Newfoundland, looks like and has the temperament of his grandfather, a "good-hearted" soul whom anyone "could fool . . . with a joke" (24). After they reach their ancestral home on Quoyle's Point, across Omaloor Bay from Killick-Claw, Quoyle learns that the bay is named for his family and that an "omaloor" is a "big, stun clumsy, witless, simple-minded type of fellow" (58). Quoyle seems to live up to this description, becoming the butt of jokes and allowing people to take advantage of his gullibility. Soon after he arrives, convinced that despite his fear of water he should have a boat for traveling the direct route back and forth from Quoyle's Point to Killick-Claw, he buys an unseaworthy boat that no one else wants, somehow failing to notice the men congratulating the owner and laughing. Billy warns Quoyle that the boat is unseaworthy, but Quoyle does not try to return it or find a better one.

Even before they leave for Newfoundland, Agnis tells Quoyle that his father, Guy Quoyle, is the product of an incestuous union of Sian Quoyle, who died at age twelve, and his sister Addy. Addy next "took up" with her brother Turvy before marrying Agnis's father, Cokey Hamm (27). Quoyle's father continued the family "tradition" by sexually abusing Agnis, beginning when she was only six and a half, a secret Agnis manages to keep from Quoyle until late in the novel. Soon after her arrival in Newfoundland, Agnis takes her revenge by dumping Guy's ashes in the privy at the house on Quoyle's Point and urinating on them.

These and other instances of incest in the Quoyle family are not the main reason for the townspeople's derision of the family. As the sexual-abuse stories in the *Gammy Bird* reveal, incest between children and older family members is widespread. In fact, it become a kind of metaphor for the Newfoundlanders' insular way of life, not only the literal interrelationships of the families but also their frequent tendency to disparage and ignore the outside world that is all too often crashing in on them.

The townspeople's Quoyle jokes are partly based on fear. One old-timer, Skipper Alfred, tells Quoyle that the family was "a savage pack," reputed to have "nailed a man to a tree by 'is ears, cut off 'is nose for the scent of blood to draw nippers and flies that devoured 'im alive" (139). Billy Pretty calls the old Quoyles "[l]oonies. . . . wild and inbred, half-wits and murderers" (162).

When Billy takes Quoyle to visit the deserted, volcanic Gaze Island—once home to the Quoyles and a handful of intermarried families, including the Prettys—Quoyle learns more about his ancestors. According to Billy, "They were wrackers they say, come to Gaze Island centuries ago and made it their evil lair." That is, they "lured ships onto the rocks" around the island by building fires to trick mariners into believing they were following signal lights to a safe harbor (171).

Quoyle is aghast at thoughts of "[a]ncestors whose filthy blood ran in his veins, who murdered the shipwrecked, drowned their unwanted brats, fought and howled" (174). Yet, as Billy has pointed out, "there was many, many people here depended on shipwrecks to improve their lot" (172), and many pirates used to come to New-foundland to hire their crews. Again the Quoyles' past crimes are more extreme than their neighbors' but not entirely different.

Quoyle's biggest discovery on his trip with Billy is that the big green house on Quoyle's Point that he and Agnis are so carefully restoring once stood on Gaze Island. In the 1880s or 1890s some fifty Quoyles and their relatives dragged the house "miles and miles across the ice" (162) followed by "a wrangle-gangle mob of islanders" driving the Quoyles away from the island not for their sexual practices or their wracking but for "their disinclination to attend Pentecostal services" (172).

On high, exposed Quoyle's Point the Quoyles moored the house to the rock with huge cables tied to iron rings. As Agnis explains, "Top of the rock not quite level . . . . Before my time, but they said it rocked in storms like a big rocking chair, back and forth. Made the women sick, afraid, so they lashed it down and it doesn't move an inch but the wind singing through those cables makes a noise you don't forget" (43). The house becomes an emblem of the family, its isolated location representing the old Quoyles' status as outsiders and its moorings suggesting their holding on to that place more by force of will than by any kinship to the surrounding com-munity. Later in the novel Quoyle realizes that regardless of how much work they do on the house it retains "its gaunt look," as though dragging it across the ice has "twisted the house out of true" (185)—an observation shared by his eerily psychic daughter Bunny. He comes to think of the house as "[a] bound prisoner straining to get free. . . . a tethered animal, dumb but feeling" (263).

By the time Quoyle discovers his ancestors' sordid past, how-ever, he and his immediate family have already established ties of

their own with the people of Killick-Claw. He has gained the friendship of his coworkers, who—having feared he would be "a big, wild
booger" (162)—have discovered that he is just big, and an easy target for a joke. Agnis has reopened her successful yacht-upholstery
business, and his daughters have established friendships with the
daughters of their sitter, Beety Buggit, who is the daughter-in-law of
Quoyle's boss and the wife of Dennis Buggit, who is helping to
repair the house at Quoyle's Point. In addition to his friendship with
Dennis and Beety, Quoyle has tentatively begun to court Wavey
Prowse, a young widow with a son who has Down syndrome.

Furthermore, Quoyle has impressed Jack with "Killer Yacht at
Killick-Claw," a story about the *Tough Baby,* a Dutch Botterjacht,
or pleasure barge, originally built for Adolf Hitler. Because he likes
the story, Jack tells Quoyle to write a regular column, "The Shipping
News," of similar stories about interesting boats. Quoyle reflects
that he is thirty-six and that Jack's praise marks "the first time any-
body ever said he'd done it right" (144).

While writing the story Quoyle "had a sense of writing well,"
feeling that the current owners' "pride in the boat's destructiveness
shone out of the piece." Silver and Bayonet Melville have told him
how their yacht came loose from its moorings in Hurricane Bob, and
survived with scarcely a scratch. It is so heavy, however, that it
destroyed seventeen other boats and reduced a dozen expensive
beach houses and their docks to "absolute rubble" (142). The
Melvilles, who have come to Newfoundland to have Agnis reuphol-
ster their yacht furnishings, are seriocomic grotesques. Their last
name suggests an invidious comparison between the rugged
mariners of the days of novelist Herman Melville and the dilettantes
who sail the seas in the 1980s. Silver's wealth comes from the off-

shore oil wells that are ruining the Newfoundland fishing grounds. The ironically named Bayonet is a former tour guide. They are arguing when Quoyle interviews them, and the *Tough Baby* later leaves port suddenly before Agnis has completed her work or been paid. Silver has murdered Bayonet and with the help of her lover has cut his body into pieces, giving new meaning to the words "Killer Yacht" in Quoyle's story. She later mails the money to Agnis from Macau, an inexplicable expression of morality that leads to her arrest.

The discovery of the murder comes when Quoyle and Billy are returning from their trip to Gaze Island. Among the rocks to which the old Quoyles once lured ships, on a particular formation called the Net-Man for its tendency to catch floating objects, Quoyle finds a suitcase with a distinctive improvised handle made from a rope tied in a knot called a "Dutch cringle," a suitcase last seen on the deck of the *Tough Baby* (174). Billy teases Quoyle about being a "wracker" like his ancestors, but after he finds Bayonet Melville's head inside the case, he is also the object of sympathy in the community, particularly from Wavey and her brother, who invites Quoyle to visit Wavey whenever he wants.

Another affirmation of Quoyle's rising professional status comes when he devotes one of his columns to the damage done to wildlife by oil spills from tankers that have not been properly maintained. Criticizing Quoyle's "bloody American pinko Greenpeace liberalism" (202), Tert rewrites the column as a paean to oil tankers. In a reaction that surprises even himself, the usually meek and passive Quoyle blows up at Tert and calls Jack, who tells Tert to leave Quoyle's columns alone. As Jack says to Quoyle, "If you put your foot in a dog's mess we'll say it's because you was brought up in the States" (204).

Whatever the faults of the Newfoundlanders in the novel, in general the greatest evils in the novel come from the outside, whether from the misguided efforts of the Canadian government or from people such as the Melvilles, who bring the senseless violence that too often seems to characterize late-twentieth-century life in the United States. Proulx drives home this point later in the novel, when Partridge calls from Los Angeles, where he has been living, to report that a crazed gunman has shot and killed several people at *The Mockingburg Record* and that his wife has been shot at on the freeway. Newfoundland is still a place apart from the modern world that is gradually encroaching on it. As Jack comments to Quoyle, "Worst you'll get here . . . is a good punch-up and maybe your car pushed over the cliff" (291). Sometimes the local practical joking goes beyond civility, however, as when the guests at a farewell party for Nutbeem destroy and sink his boat in an attempt to keep him from leaving. Nutbeem is surprisingly accepting of his loss, but he leaves anyway, by airplane.

Writing in 1997 about her first impressions of the Great Northern Peninsula, Proulx described how she "felt a supernatural alertness to the landscape."[6] Quoyle too begins to discover some of the magic of the place and its people. Proulx also wrote of a later trip to the area, during which a conversation with a husband and wife turned to a favorite Newfoundland subject: stories about "strange events, anomalous days and eerie, inexplicable happenings." After Proulx began telling about her own strange experience, the husband completed her story in "frighteningly accurate" detail.[7]

Quoyle has not been in Newfoundland long before he learns that his employer, Jack Buggit, has a similar kind of second sight. Jack senses when people are in trouble at sea. He knew right away when his elder son was drowned. When his second son, Dennis, and another sailor were lost at sea, and the coast guard called off the search, Jack went out by himself and found them. "How he knew where to go is beyond logic" (97), says Nutbeem. Jack is more than a benevolent father figure using story assignments to help Quoyle and the other reporters. As the novel progresses he takes on nearly mythic proportions, using his extraordinary perceptiveness to work good among his people.

While Jack sometimes seems to be employing a kind of "white magic," there is "black magic" at work in the novel as well. Its practitioner is Nolan Quoyle, the last of the old Quoyles, who resents the return of Agnis and Quoyle to reclaim a place that their cousin Nolan considers rightfully, if not legally, his own. He first became an outcast because the men with whom he fished considered him a jinx on their fishing weather, calling him "Squally Quoyle" (297). Later, according to Billy, Nolan is reputed to have had sex with his wife's corpse.

When Quoyle and his family reach Quoyle's Point for the first time, Bunny, who shares Jack's gift, sees Nolan's "strange dog, white, somehow misshapen" (46) and senses the presence of evil. She develops a phobia about white dogs and frightens her father and aunt by imagining she sees the dog at times when they cannot. Eventually Agnis comes to suspect that Bunny might be "sensitive in a way the rest of us aren't," explaining to Quoyle, "There's people like that here" (134).

Even after he begins to see the old man and his dog lurking about the house and after Billy warns that Nolan is "the old style of Quoyle, stealthy in the night" (161), Quoyle does not immediately understand Nolan's malicious intentions. Nor does he understand the significance of the knotted bits of grass and twine he begins finding around his house.

Nolan is practicing an ancient form of magic. Sir James George Frazer's *The Golden Bough* (1890–1915), a groundbreaking work on comparative religion and mythology, records instances of traditional societies that believed in the power of tying and untying knots to work good as well as evil. Cyrus Lawrence Day in his *Quipus and Witches' Knots: The Role of the Knot in Primitive and Ancient Cultures* (1967), a book from which Proulx quotes in the headnote to chapter 23, includes further details on the magic of knots. Proulx's Newfoundlanders continue to practice this form of superstitious magic. Tert Card, for example, wears "knot charms" against canker sores, but has them anyway (198). Nolan, in contrast, uses knots as curses and specializes in tying and untying them to conjure up winds and storms, a practice Frazer described in some detail. While Proulx leaves open the question of whether Nolan's magic is the literal cause of any of the events in the novel, Nolan clearly believes in it, and it most certainly functions on a symbolic level, giving ominous overtones to the knots described in chapter headings and used by various characters.

The chapter in which Quoyle and Agnis see Nolan lurking near their house and discuss whether they should establish contact with the old man is headed with a quotation from Day's *Quipus and Witches' Knots:* "The mysterious power that is supposed to reside in knots . . . can be injurious as well as beneficial" (185). Agnis, who knew Nolan during her early years in Newfoundland, is emphatic in her refusal to "ferret out some old fourth cousin with a grudge" (188).

Jack's and Nolan's forms of magic come together in chapter 26, "Deadman," which includes one of the most important scenes in the book. Home alone on a September afternoon, Quoyle, who has just absentmindedly picked up and pocketed one of Nolan's knotted pieces of twine, sees the body of a man caught in a dog-shaped rock at the end of the point. Thinking there might be a chance to save the man, Quoyle sets out on rough waters in his unseaworthy boat. As his inexperience gets him in trouble, he notices a piece of line that has been placed in the boat: "It was knotted at one end, kinked and crimped at the other as if old knots had finally been untied. For the first time Quoyle got it—there was meaning in knotted strings" (210). Yet, he does not accept the fate Nolan has apparently intended for him. The boat capsizes, but in the space of "fifteen terrifying seconds" he discovers he can swim and, thinking that it is "stupid to drown with the children so small," he manages to stay afloat for hours by clinging to an empty cooler from his boat (211). He is finally rescued by Jack, who exclaims, "I *knowed* somebody was out here. Felt it" (212). The scene is important for its demonstration of the power of good Newfoundland "magic" over bad, but, even more significant for Quoyle, it indicates the extent to which he has learned to take control of his own destiny and to have confidence in his ability to do so. Furthermore, the body turns out to be the rest of Bayonet Melville's dismembered corpse, a grisly reminder of the outside influences that threaten the Newfoundlanders' way of life.

Jack is not the only force opposing Nolan's magic. Quoyle's thoughts of his daughters at a time when he is near death suggest their positive motivation in his life. Bunny, with her seemingly psychic powers, has a particularly important role. In *Quipus and Witches' Knots,* Day points out that "the supposed effectiveness of a magic knot depends as much on the intentions of the person who ties the knot as on the virtues of the knot itself" and that the same

knot might be harmful or beneficial.[8] A few months after his near
drowning, Bunny shows Quoyle "The Sun Clouded Over," a cat's
cradle figure that Skipper Alfred has taught her—a figure that Day
dates back to the ancient Greeks—which she is making with a piece
of knotted string that Nolan left on the back of the driver's seat in
Quoyle's car. On the metaphorical, and magical, level of the novel,
Bunny is altering, or modifying the magic that Nolan has made with
his knots, though, indeed, they are still there. The local people recognize Bunny's psychic powers. As Agnis's employee Mavis Bangs
points out, Bunny is "a real Quoyle, tilted like a buoy in a raging
sea" (180). Yet, though she may be difficult and at times disturbing,
she is a loving child who is fiercely loyal to her family—even her
extended family, as she proves when she gets in trouble at school for
knocking down a teacher who has been unkind to Wavey's son,
Herry, and made him cry. Bunny not only recognizes Nolan's magic
early, but her love is a force against it.

Soon after his boating accident Quoyle decides to take the girls
to live in town for the winter, realizing the difficulty he will have
traveling to and from Killick-Claw by land or sea in snowy weather.
While Agnis and her helpers are working at a big job in St. John's,
he and his daughters become part of the social structure of Killick-
Claw. When Tert leaves to edit a newsletter for an oil company, Jack
surprises everyone by making Quoyle managing editor.

Quoyle's personal successes are clouded by Nolan, however,
who continues to practice his knot "magic." When Quoyle goes to
the house at Quoyle's Point alone one day and finds pieces of knotted twine at the thresholds of all the bedrooms, he becomes enraged
at the implied threat to his children and decides to confront the old
man. Never having talked to Nolan before or even seen him up

close, Quoyle finds him living in abject poverty in nearby Capsize
Cove. Despite the old man's dirty, disheveled appearance, Quoyle
recognizes Nolan's family resemblance (including Quoyle's own
jutting chin). In this first face-to-face meeting with the last old-style
Quoyle, he learns something else as well: "In the man before him in
the hut, crammed with the poverty of another century, Quoyle saw
what he had sprung from. For the old man was mad, the gears of his
mind stripped long ago to clashing discs edged with the stubs of broken cogs. Mad with loneliness or lovelessness, or from some genetic
chemical jumble, or the flooding betrayal that all hermits suffer"
(264). When Quoyle throws the knotted strings on the floor, Nolan
quickly throws them into the wood stove, claiming that the knots are
now "fixed by fire" and can never be undone. Even with this threat
of continued curses, Quoyle is moved by sympathy for the old man
"[w]hose last pathetic defense against imagined enemies was to tie
a knot in a bit of string" (265).

Having reached some understanding of this living remnant of
his family's history, Quoyle has yet another step to take before he
can exorcise its demons: he must accept his responsibility for his
kinsman, no matter how distasteful he may find the old man. Dennis Buggit calls Quoyle's attention to this obligation shortly after
Christmas. When they visit Nolan, they find him barely alive in a
reeking house, "too weak or befuddled to get to the outhouse" and
burning the walls of his house for firewood (282). At Dennis's suggestion Quoyle, feeling guilty about not having done something to
help the wretched man earlier, puts Nolan in a mental hospital in St.
John's, while Dennis mercifully drowns the half-dead white dog.

When Quoyle visits Nolan in the hospital, the old man at first
seems fairly lucid and grateful for clean clothing and good food.

Confessing to Quoyle that he "tied knots 'gainst you. Raised winds" (296), he apologizes for his actions and seems harmless. When Quoyle returns the next day, however, he learns that the old man has gone on a violent rampage and had to be sedated. Though he is physically out of Quoyle's life, Nolan continues to tie knots against him. One April night, during a particularly violent storm that seems to come from nowhere, Nolan lies in his bed at the hospital happy "at what he had conjured with wind-knots" (318). At the same time Bunny, asleep in the house Quoyle has rented in Killick-Claw, has a particularly vivid dream vision of the house at Quoyle's Point breaking free from its cables and blowing away. The next day Wavey's father shows Quoyle through his binoculars that the house at Quoyle's Point is gone.

The novel remains noncommital about whether the storm was caused by Nolan's latest black-magic attempt to curse his cousins or by some random meteorological phenomenon. In fact, the loss of the house—which has unpleasant associations for Quoyle and Agnis, despite her sentimental attachment to it—may be seen as a liberating experience, leaving them free to strengthen the ties they are developing in town. There is one way, however, in which Nolan does manage to hurt his cousins—through the simple, nonsupernatural vehicle of talk.

An extremely private person, Agnis has two secrets that she plans to keep from Quoyle and her friends in Killick-Claw at all costs: that from an early age she was repeatedly raped by Quoyle's father and that her dear friend and life companion, Warren, to whom she lovingly refers throughout the novel, was actually Irene Warren, Agnis's long-time lesbian lover. During Quoyle's visit to the hospital Nolan talks about Agnis's coming to Nolan's mother for help in aborting Guy's baby, thus revealing one of Agnis's secrets. Later, while they are discussing what to do about their vanished house, Quoyle lets slip that Nolan has told him her secret, deeply wounding Agnis, who decides she can no longer live with Quoyle, "[w]ho knew what he knew" (323). Making up plans as she talks, she suggests that they use the house insurance money to build a summer camp at Quoyle's Point while Quoyle can buy the house he has been renting in town and she can fix up an apartment over the shop with Mavis Bangs, who has asked to buy a partnership in the upholstery business. Even Nolan's final curse, then, has an effect opposite to his intentions. Instead of driving his cousins away, he pushes them into the arms of the community.

The greatest burden Quoyle has to overcome is neither the stigma of his family history nor his lack of confidence in his professional abilities. Rather, it is the romanticized fiction he has created about his marriage to Petal. Wavey too was married to an unfaithful spouse who made no attempt to hide his philandering from her. Like Quoyle, she is devoted to a romanticized vision of that spouse, which she created as a kindness to her child but seems to have come to believe herself. Faithful to Herold Prowse's memory, she holds Quoyle at arm's length. On an autumn berry-picking expedition, when he takes her in his arms for the first time, she begins to yield but then remembers "Herold's handsome bones tangled in ghost nets," and pushes Quoyle away (195). Even after they have sex with each other for the first time, when Wavey goes to St. John's with Quoyle in late January so he can visit Nolan in the hospital, she observes as she lies in his arms that she and Herold spent their honeymoon at the same hotel. Quoyle also fights the possibility that he might be in love again. Still convinced that he will never love any woman but Petal, he "equate[s] misery with love," and when he is with Wavey he feels only "comfort and a modest joy" (304). By March, however, he and Wavey are able to tell one another the truth about their spouses, leading to an exchange in which Quoyle explains a realization that has come to him quite recently: "Petal wasn't any good. And I think maybe that's why I loved her." Wavey responds, "Same with Herold. It's like you feel to yourself that's all you deserve" (308).

Not long afterward, on a picnic with Wavey, Agnis, and all three children, Quoyle remembers how Billy Pretty has told him that his father "[u]sed to say there was four women in every man's heart. The Maid in the Meadow, the Demon Lover, the Stouthearted Woman, the Tall and Quiet Woman" (171). He realizes that his daughters are his Maids in the Meadow, while the other roles are filled by Petal, Agnis, and Wavey, respectively. Yet he wonders, "If he and Wavey married, would Petal be in the bed with them? Or Herold Prowse? He imagined the demon lovers coupling, biting and growling, while he and Wavey crouched against the footboard with their eyes squeezed shut, fingers in their ears" (314). At his party to welcome Agnis back to Killick-Claw, held on the night of the storm that blows their house away, he tentatively develops a new definition of love: perhaps it is "like a bag of assorted sweets passed around from which one might choose more than once" (315). Though he knows he will never have the passion for Wavey that he had for Petal, he kisses Wavey in front of all the guests, an action "[a]s good as an announcement" (316).

Quoyle's happiness in his new life is apparent in his new self-image. More overweight than ever, he sees his naked body in a full-length mirror as he is climbing out of the tub one night. He recognizes that he has become "immense," but decides that "the effect was more of strength than obesity. He guessed he was at some prime physical point. Middle age was not too far ahead, but it didn't frighten him. It was harder to count his errors now, perhaps because they had compounded beyond counting or blurred into his general condition." As he puts on his nightshirt, "a bolt of joy passed through him. For no reason" (327). Unlike Loyal in *Postcards,* whose failure to examine his life makes him more and more grotesque and nonhuman, Quoyle starts out as a laughable, grotesque failure and, through his attempts to come to terms with his past and take control of his life, becomes a confident, compassionate human being. While he is still given to self-delusion and is indeed larger than ever, by this late point in *The Shipping News* he has become like a giant in a comic epic.

Though the novel never crosses into the realm of magical realism, as it progresses it increasingly approaches the line between fiction and pure fantasy. The climactic scene of the novel—Jack Buggit's "death" and "resurrection"—comes closest to that boundary. Out on his boat alone, Jack has thrown a lobster trap overboard, caught his foot in the rope, and been jerked overboard. As he reached for his knife, the knot on the cord that attached it to his belt slipped and the knife falls away, leaving him stranded under water with no way to free himself. When he is finally found, efforts to resuscitate him fail, and Billy brings the body home, where his wife and her sisters prepare it for burial. At the wake, however, Jack suddenly sits up in his coffin and starts coughing. After several weeks recovering from pneumonia, he is as healthy as ever and remembers that as he slipped into a coma underwater he "came to believe vividly that he was in an enormous pickle jar. Waiting for someone to draw him out" (336).

Since there have been medically documented cases of people who have survived long periods of immersion in cold water and since Jack's body was prepared for burial at home and not embalmed, his resurrection is plausible, if surprising. Yet it also adds to the aura of mythic grandeur that has gradually surrounded him in the course of the novel. If Quoyle is the good giant in this modern epic, Jack is the wise magician-king, who like those described by Frazer, uses his magic and so-called supernatural powers for the good of his people.

The adults in the novel accept the explanation that Jack was not dead, just in a coma, but his reawakening means something different to Bunny. When Petal died, Quoyle, like many well-meaning adults, attempted to explain death to his daughters by telling them that it is like sleep. As a result, the hypersensitive Bunny has not only had nightmares but also believes that she can return to New York someday and wake up her mother. When she asks to go to Jack's wake, which she calls "the awake" (331), Quoyle is uncertain about letting the girls attend, but Wavey argues that they need to learn about the reality of death, to distinguish it from sleep. Jack's sudden awakening, of course, has the opposite effect from what Wavey intended. Bunny is more sure than ever that death is just sleep after she and Wavey return to a rock where they left a dead bird before the big storm. Despite Wavey's rational explanations that the bird could have been blown away or eaten by an animal, Bunny is sure the bird "flew away" (336).

The novel ends on this note of fantasy at the wedding of Wavey and Quoyle, who muses, "[I]f Jack Buggit could escape from the pickle jar, if a bird with a broken neck could fly away, what else might be possible? Water may be older than light, diamonds crack in hot goat's blood, mountaintops give off cold fire, forests appear in midocean, it may happen that a crab is caught with the shadow of a hand on its back, that the wind be imprisoned in a bit of knotted string. And it may be that love sometimes occurs without pain and misery" (336–37). The phrasing of this beautifully lyrical passage is conditional rather than absolute, and much of what Quoyle posits seems unlikely to be true in an objective sense, suggesting to the reader that he has substituted new illusions for old. As Proulx has noted, this conclusion "defines happiness as the absence of pain,"[9] offering a far more qualified affirmation than some reviewers found in the novel. Yet, in the fog-wrapped mythical Newfoundland of the novel, all the things Quoyle mentions seem possible.

The Shipping News also warns of the danger inherent in ignoring events outside the inward-looking island world of Newfoundland. The traditional culture that Proulx documents so vividly through the stories and actions of major and minor characters has already undergone change because of the intrusion of outside forces and the exodus of many Newfoundlanders to mainland Canada in search of work. Few return, and, as Quoyle learns, those who do are "altered in temper as a knife reclaimed from the ashes of a house fire" and thus "lost forever" to those who have stayed behind (326).

The result of Canada giving fishing rights to other countries, which send large fishing trawlers to the Grand Banks off Newfoundland, is a depletion of the fish and shellfish populations, which particularly hurts the local fishermen, who fish closer to the shoreline of the island than the big trawlers. The depletion has also resulted in strict licensing restrictions. If Jack ever stops renewing his salmon and lobster licenses, he can never get them again, and the only way Dennis Buggit can get any kind of license is for his father to sign one over to him or leave it to him. (After Jack's entanglement with the lobster trap, he lets Dennis have his lobstering license, thus making it possible for his son to stay in Killick-Claw instead of reluctantly moving to Toronto in search of work.)

Another traditional source of income for Newfoundlanders is seal hunting, which is strongly opposed by environmental groups worldwide. Proulx's description of Jack's annual seal hunt presents a far different picture from that seen on television footage shot by environmentalists. Jack's method is humane; his take is limited; and seal hunting is presented as a source not only of pelts for rich women's coats but also of food for the islanders.

Another source of protein for the Newfoundlanders' diet is the moose, a species not indigenous to the island but brought there around the time of the First World War. As Wavey explains to Quoyle, "The Gandy Goose," the song her uncle Alvin Yark sings incessantly, refers to the *Bruce,* a ship carrying moose that sank off the coast of Newfoundland. Alvin Yark practices another traditional craft, boatbuilding, going into the woods and choosing just the right trees every time he starts a new one. He explains to Quoyle that he never uses dry wood, which soaks up water when the boat is launched. Instead he builds his boats "with green wood and water will never go into the wood" (237). Later, after he has found the perfect spruce tree to use as the stem for "a lean boat, not too lean," for Quoyle, Alvin explains, "Each tree grows a little different so every boat you make, you know, the rake of the stem and the rake of the stern is a little different too, and that makes it so you 'as different 'ulls. Each one is different, like men and women, some good, some not so good" (265–66). As Proulx explained in 1997, because some parts of boats are curved, a good boatbuilder had to have "a practiced eye that could see these shapes in crooked trunks, roots and branches."[10] Believing that steaming boards to bend them produces an inferior boat, Alvin has an intimate knowledge of his materials that is becoming increasingly rare in the modern world. Proulx, however, found evidence of its value when she bought a 105-year-old house in Newfoundland. Even though much of its structure was rotting away, the house stood straight and square because its builders had cut "stern knee shapes from spruce, most likely where a trunk bent into a root,"[11] and put eight of these strong naturally right-angled pieces at the corners of the house.

Jack's job history before he started the *Gammy Bird* is an example of how little such traditional skills are valued in the modern world. After he could no longer make a living at fishing and sealing, Canada Manpower promised to retrain him and found him a job at a tannery that ran out of hides and closed after a few months. Next they sent him to work at an industrial-machinery plant that never opened and then at a cardboard-liner factory that closed after three months. Finally a big glove factory was built near Quoyle's Point, and ferry service was set up to cross Omaloor Bay to and from Killick-Claw. Jack was one of many who took the ferry to work at the factory on opening day, only to discover that there was no leather with which to make gloves. As he explains to Quoyle, the leather was supposed to come from the tannery that folded, but "nobody ever told the guys building the glove factory, nobody ever told Canada Manpower" (67). The factory never opened, and the ferry stopped service after its second run, back to Killick-Claw.

Proulx depicts Newfoundland, which did not become part of Canada until 1949, as having been ill served by giving up much of its autonomy to a large confederation governed by politicians whose decisions seem based on ignorance of the island and its people. Yet she also suggests that too many of those people rely on television as the main source of news about the outside world, ignoring it at their own peril. Like Proulx's other novels, *The Shipping News* makes a plea for respecting and preserving all that is good in the traditional lifestyles and the natural and cultural heritage before they are lost forever. It is also a warning not to underestimate the forces of change that threaten them. As Proulx explains, not long after the novel was completed, the cod stock in the region became so depleted that the Canadian government issued a fishing moratorium that essentially destroyed the Newfoundland fishing economy.[12]

CHAPTER FIVE

Accordion Crimes

Proulx's third novel, *Accordion Crimes* (1996), continues her examination of people living against the background of historical change. This time she broadens her focus to a period of roughly a century in American life, from the 1890s into the 1990s. To suggest the long-term implications of the lives and events she describes in each of the eight sections, Proulx employs a device she calls a "flash-forward" to sketch briefly the fates of selected characters beyond the time frame of the story. Though the sections include information about the past and future histories of families, each one focuses on a different period in American history: the anti-immigrant, anti-Catholic period of the late nineteenth century, particularly as its sentiments were expressed in the anti-Italian riots of 1891 in New Orleans; the era of the First World War, with its rising tide of anti-German sentiment; the economic boom time of the Second World War and its immediate aftermath, which ended the Great Depression of the 1930s and increased social and geographic mobility; and every succeeding decade into the 1990s, as characters live their lives against the backdrop of events such as the civil rights movement and the Vietnam War and social trends such as the ever-increasing urbanization of the American population and the homogenization of American culture through the pervasive influence of the mass media.

In its scope and in its theme of individuals at the mercy of historical forces beyond their understanding or control, Proulx's third novel, like her first, has much in common with John Dos Passos's

U.S.A. trilogy (1930–1936). She too grapples with the threads of U.S. history in an ambitious attempt to weave a definition of the American experience.

A major casualty in Proulx's definition is the idealistic view of the United States as a "melting pot" in which all races and ethnic groups are assimilated into a single prejudice-free "American" culture—a myth Proulx is not the first to debunk. Popularized during the early decades of the twentieth century by Israel Zangwill's play *The Melting Pot* (1909), this view is well illustrated by a movie featuring "an enormous black kettle" that one of Proulx's characters sees in the 1920s: "Into one side of the kettle danced clots of immigrants in old-country costumes, singing in foreign tongues and kicking their legs, and out the other side marched a row of Americans in suits, whistling 'The Star-Spangled Banner.'"[1] Historically, as in Proulx's novel, much of this acculturation took place in public school classrooms, where teachers forced the children of recent immigrants to speak English and disparaged the cultural practices of the children's families. The "American" culture with which newcomers were supposed to replace their own was that of the first European immigrants to the East Coast of North America, white Anglo-Saxon Protestants. Indeed, non-Protestant immigrants found little tolerance for their religions. As one German-American character jokes, "You know why the Puritans left England for America? . . . Jesus Christ, like the feller says, it was so they could carry on their religion in freedom and force others to do the same" (68).

While melting pot acculturation was never as successful as its advocates hoped, many children of immigrants (and their children after them) did lose touch with the languages and cultures of their parents' homelands as they were taught to disparage their heritage and engaged in the headlong rush to redefine themselves as "Americans." Proulx has described *Accordion Crimes* as an attempt to examine "the American penchant for redefining the self, our attraction to shape-shifting, career changes, plastic surgery and cosmetic makeover, sex changes, our root-tearing mobility"; moreover, she wonders if the reason for this national characteristic might be "the immigrant experience, the rite of passage of literally redefining oneself as an American."[2] *Accordion Crimes* offers evidence to support this hypothesis.

Another theme of the novel is racial, ethnic, and religious bigotry—one of the least admirable aspects of the American experience. As successive waves of Europeans arrived in the nineteenth century—mainly from Britain, Ireland, Germany, and Scandinavia in the 1840s through the 1870s, but in growing numbers from eastern and southern Europe during the 1880s and 1890s—they brought their own prejudices along with their cultures, and learned new biases in the United States. In Europe they had little experience in dealing with people of other nationalities. Moreover, they often tended to identify themselves as a member of an ethnic group within their own nationality. Two modern European nations were so new that immigrants from Italy and Germany, both unified in 1871 after decades of strife and territorial gains, still tended to think of themselves as natives of the smaller states that formed those nations. The immigrant from Sicily in part 1 of *Accordion Crimes* is surprised to discover that "Americans believe Sicilians and Italians are the same and hate them both." In fact, he and his son are warned not only to learn English quickly but also "to cast aside their Sicilian dialect" and speak Italian because "Italians say Sicilians speak thieves' language in order to plot murder in their open faces" (26). The three

Germans in the second section of the novel are unified by their love of German language and culture, but they left Europe as a Württemberger, a Saxon, and a Königsberger (from East Prussia) and "became Germans in America" (55). The accordion player from Poland, a country fought over and divided by Germany and Russia for centuries, looks down on fellow countrymen from the Tatra Mountain region as uncultured Polish "hillbillies."

In large part the children of European immigrants gradually cast aside their prejudices toward each other, instead focusing their bigotry on the next group of newcomers. *Accordion Crimes* is not only the fictionalized history of the American immigrant experience but also the story of the myriad forms of bigotry that have accompanied it. The novel is full of offensive and no doubt authentic ethnic jokes aimed at one group after another. The most striking thing about them is how often they seem interchangeable. Proulx emphasizes this point in the final section of the novel, when one man tells a joke about a black man lynched in Alaska and another says he has heard the same joke about a Chippewa in the South. As animosities shift from one nationality to the next, the level of hatred remains constant.

While hatred holds steady, many of the positive aspects of American ethnic heritage are lost. One of the shifts Proulx portrays is the change in cooking. For example, she contrasts authentic Mexican, Cajun, and Polish cooking using fresh ingredients with bland "American" dishes made by younger, Americanized women using canned foods and various mixes filled with salt, preservatives, and artificial colorings.

One of the greatest losses in the rush to Americanization is the gradual disappearance of the folk music traditions that were brought to the United States and gradually modified to fit immigrant experiences in the New World. Proulx depicts changes in ethnic cultures through the music that different characters play on a little green accordion (and later other accordions) as the instrument passes from one owner to the next over the span of a century. As the sociologist Graeme Smith has pointed out, the accordion has traditionally been the instrument of choice in working-class cultures, whose music "provided ways of working out emotionally satisfying compromises with the contradictory and uneven progress of modernisation to which emigration had exposed so many."[3]

Characters play a large variety of accordions, as well as their musical cousin the concertina and the South American bandoneon. The green accordion is a nineteen-button, diatonic instrument, meaning that it plays the tones of the seven-note major scale. Other accordions in the novel are chromatic, playing an octave of twelve semitones, including sharps and flats not in the diatonic scale. The novel includes a wide variety of button accordions, some more complex than the green accordion, as well as piano accordions, with keyboards instead of buttons—showing how the instrument has evolved. To help the reader in visualizing the instruments, the half-title page for each section includes a picture of a different type of accordion.

"The Accordion Maker"

The first section of the novel describes the experience of the Sicilian who makes the little green accordion and dreams of life in "La Merica" (17). He hopes to have a music store in New York City and repair musical instruments. His wife, however, does not want to leave their poverty-stricken village and becomes totally paralyzed shortly before their journey, so the accordion maker takes only his eleven-year-old son, Silvano, and sets out to join his wife's brother in New York, promising to return for his wife and daughters in three years. (His wife recovers from her psychosomatic affliction not long after his departure.)The year is 1891, and immigrants are leaving Sicily by the thousands, "pouring out as cornmeal from a ripped sack" (21).

On the train to Palermo the accordion maker meets a man who is probably one of the recruiters hired by American businesses to attract cheap labor to their localities. Recognizing a greenhorn, the man easily convinces the accordion maker that he should go to New Orleans, where the weather is warm, Sicilians are welcome, and jobs are plentiful.

On shipboard the accordion maker learns that Sicilians are not as loved in New Orleans as he has been led to believe. When he and Silvano arrive there they find that the only work available for Italians and Sicilians is as poorly paid longshoremen. The job includes housing in a filthy tenement typical of the living conditions most new immigrants found in American cities well into the twentieth century. They share a tiny cubbyhole with another man and use a privy that has not been emptied in so long that "the mound of excrement protruded from the hole" (29).

The accordion maker soon learns the hierarchy of dock workers: "The Irish and the black men, the cotton screwmen, had the highest-paid work; Sicilians and Italians had to take what was left, the longshoreman jobs, but at least they were better off than the roustabouts, all black men." The accordion maker can see that the blacks' "so-called freedom was a mockery," but on the docks the black screwmen are "as good as anyone and better than immigrants." The "crafty Americans," concludes the accordion maker, are good at playing these various groups against each other (31).

The man whose fruit the accordion maker unloads, however, stands as a shining example of what he hopes to achieve. Frank Archivi, known as Signor Banana and "a Rockefeller of fruit" (31), was born to poor Sicilian parents in New Orleans. Now he owns a shipping line, controls the fruit trade from Latin America, has important political connections, and is a member of New Orleans high society.

At first the accordion maker seems to be getting ahead in life. He visits the local bars and hears jazz, the first of several authentic American-hybrid music forms in the novel, played by black musicians from the docks. He dislikes this "confused music" played with "wandering imprecision" (35–36). When he plays his own music, however, only his fellow Sicilians seem interested, "hungry to hear the lost music" that makes them grieve for home (37). But later in the evening a black musician and dock worker named Apollo, asks about the accordion, and before long he has hired the accordion maker to make him an instrument like it. Having saved some money from his job and anticipating the money Apollo will pay him, the accordion maker begins to believe that his dream of owning a music shop is within reach. At this point, however, the forces of history intervene.

The accordion maker and his son arrived in the United States at a high point of nationwide anti-Catholic and anti-Italian sentiment. The American Protective Association, formed from several smaller anti-Catholic groups in 1887, warned that the pope was at the head of a secret Catholic conspiracy to take over the government of the United States. An article in the December 1890 issue of *Popular Science Monthly,* "What Shall We Do with the Dago?," charged that

Italian immigrants were criminals who would not be deterred by American laws because even the living conditions in U.S. jails were better than those they experienced at home. The atmosphere was especially tense in New Orleans, where two Italian businessmen, Joseph Provenzano and Carlo Matranga, were involved in a dispute over control of hiring longshoremen to unload the fruit boats coming from Central America. In May 1890 gunmen hired by Provenzano fired on longshoremen employed by Matranga, with deaths resulting on both sides. The Provenzano gunmen were convicted of murder, but later granted a new trial. At that point the New Orleans police chief, David Hennessey, announced that he would testify in their behalf, claiming that Matranga was bringing to New Orleans Italian and Sicilian members of a crime syndicate known as the Mafia or Black Hand, and that more than one hundred of them were working for Matranga as longshoremen. On 15 October 1890, a week before the trial, Hennessy was shot dead in a New Orleans street.

In the midst of widespread hysteria about Mafia terrorism, the New Orleans police rounded up scores of Italians. Nineteen men, many but not all of whom worked for Matranga, were tried for the chief's murder. Though Matranga was arrested, charges against him were dropped for lack of evidence. While some of the men may have been guilty, others were in all likelihood innocent. After a trial in which witnesses were threatened and jurors bribed, the jury was undecided about three of the men and found the others not guilty. For their own protection the judge remanded the men to prison, where two days after the verdict a mob headed by a prominent New Orleans lawyer entered the prison, shot nine of the former defendants, and hanged two from lampposts. When asked his opinion of these lynchings, the mayor of New Orleans responded, "These men deserved killing and they were punished by peaceful, law abiding citizens."[4] Eight of the men killed were American citizens.

In Proulx's fictionalized version of these events, the accordion maker and Silvano, who work for one of the Matrangas, are arrested in the general round-up of Italian dock workers after the murder of the police chief. Because they are carrying weapons for self-defense and the accordion maker's poor English makes it impossible for him to understand his interrogators or answer their questions, they are held for trial. "This is the land of justice," the accordion maker tells his son, believing the police will discover their innocence and free them (40). Archivi, who is also under arrest, despite his political and social connections, has a different view: "This filthy America is fraud and deceit. My fortune is lost. America is a place of lies and bitter disappointment" (41).

After the trial and acquittals, the scene shifts to the home of a wealthy New Orleans businessman who displays the attitudes of the class that benefits from racial animosity. Pinse would rather hire "niggers than dago socialist rabble" (41) and believes that the Irish and the Italians are "dirty, diseased and dangerous incendiaries" who do not "know their place" (43). He is convinced that the Black Hand has killed the police chief and wonders why New Orleans businessmen once encouraged immigrants to come there from Italy. "The dominant American class must assert itself or lose everything" to the "mongrels of Europe," he believes (46).

As this "cultured" and "civilized" man leaves his house to join the lynch mob—a mixture of prominent men and the "rabble" they have aroused with their call for "justice"—one of his stable hands calls him to see a "rat king": a huge circle of nearly twenty rats whose tails have become so entangled that none can escape. He thinks of this rat king as he and others fire into the crowd of Italian prisoners, and he sees no difference. The true "rat king," however, is the lynch mob that prominent men have called together to do their killing for them, men easily manipulated by racial hatred and tied together by the passions of the moment. The accordion maker and Archivi are among those murdered. As Pinse walks home later, a man approaches him to invest in a new non-Italian fruit company to take over Archivi's trade—an example of how the "crafty Americans" have manipulated racial and ethnic hatreds for the sake of profit.

Silvano escapes through the kindness of a guard. As the penniless boy thinks of his dead father and his family in faraway Sicily, he begins to hate his "foolish, weak Sicilian father who had failed to learn American ways and let himself be killed" (50). The first of Proulx's characters to redefine himself, he takes the "American" name Bob Joe, casts aside the language and customs of Sicily, and finds a job on a shrimp boat. When he is older, Proulx reveals in a flash-forward, he works as a roustabout in oil and gas fields, ending up in Venezuela, "where his game ended as he crouched in the jungle trying to relieve himself and a hostile Indian's arrow pierced his throat" (25).

When the accordion maker was arrested, he entrusted his little green accordion to Apollo, who gets a job working on lumber boats upriver, taking the instrument with him. He is murdered by another waterman, who takes the accordion and heads upstream.

"The Goat Gland Operation"

In the second section of *Accordion Crimes* the reader learns that Apollo's murderer has sold the little green accordion to a lumberyard owner when the wood boat on which he was working stopped

at Keokuk, Iowa. There, in 1893, the instrument is bought by Hans
Beutle, who earlier that year founded the town of Prank, Iowa, with
two other Germans, Ludwig Messermacher and William Loats.

In naming the town the other men deferred to Beutle, who
chose *Pranken* (the German word for "forepaws") because he
thought the name should "show the work of our hands" in building
their farms and the town. On the papers filed at the county seat, however, the name was written as "Prank." As Loats complains, "Your
life becomes a joke because language mixes up!" (59).

By the end of September, when Beutle buys the accordion for
a dollar, the industrious Germans are established on their farms.
Beutle starts talking about forming a band with the other men and
builds a *Bierstube* (beer garden) under the willow trees where the
Little Runt River runs through his farm. He misses the music and
conviviality of such places in Germany and says that "Americans
understand nothing of how to live, only to get and get and get" (62).
Historically this difference tended to be a source of friction between
German immigrants and those who preceded them. Descendants of
the early Puritan settlers admired the Germans' frugality and indus-
triousness, but they disapproved of their beer drinking and musical
festivities, particularly because they often took place on Sundays.

By 1900 the building of railroad lines through Prank has
brought Irish laborers to lay the tracks and a fresh spate of ethnic and
religious prejudice. Though he is happy to take board money from
four Irish workers while they live in his house for a year, Beutle calls
them dirty, whiskey-drinking Catholics who commit crimes
"because they can go to confession, a few prayers and zack! All is
wiped clean" (65). Beutle, Louts, and Messermacher, however, are
"freethinkers, self-confessed agnostics who bragged that there was

not a bible among them" (74), and their beliefs are as unpopular with others as Catholicism is with them. At the Fourth of July celebration the Irish snigger at Beutle's heavy German accent while he delivers a speech to celebrate the completion of the second railroad line. Later as the three Germans play comic German songs and polkas until midnight, the Irish "shouted for jigs and reels the Germans could not play, and the Americans wanted 'Old Ned Tupper' and 'Arkansas Traveler'" (67).

Some of the Irish railroad workers stay behind in Prank and prosper. The increased proximity of different cultures brings more animosity than understanding. Beutle becomes more and more strident in his insistence on the superiority of everything German. He reveals the depth of his prejudice one day as he is driving a troupe of gypsies off his land at shotgun point and shoots an old woman in the rump because he thinks she is moving too slowly. When his children protest his cruelty, he shouts, "[F]oreigners is animals, they don't feel pain" (68), forgetting that he was once a foreigner himself and is still perceived as one by many.

Having always said that German accordions are superior to his little Italian instrument, Beutle eventually buys a Hohner accordion with "a bright aggressive German tone" and gives the green accordion to Messermacher so they can start an accordion band. Their music is "good loud farmers' music and the way to dance to it was to stamp" (70). It is not admired by everyone in town but it remains in demand for a time.

As the Germans cease to dominate Prank society, they start to become the butt of local jokes. Lusty Beutle has been seen having sex with his wife out of doors and receives pornographic photographs in the mail. Townspeople laugh when they hear Beutle's name and joke that perhaps all the Germans' children have really been fathered by Beutle. They speak of "German beasts" in the same tone that Beutle used to describe the gypsies.

By 1910 the three Germans seem as immersed in their German heritage as ever, joining the German-American Historical Society in a predominantly German town about thirty miles away, where Beutle gives a speech—not entirely based on fact—about German Americans' many contributions to the United States. The Railway Express man in Prank has a different perspective: "[B]etter drown them all—they can't never fit this country, the Dutchies, those square-heads, those sourkrauts" (73).

Their claims of superiority have clearly hurt the Germans, but so has their success. Their farms are "showplaces," and even when people around lose everything, the three Germans manage to grow good crops. Fueled by jealousy, as well as by stories about Beutle, rumors spread about "German lubricity and incest." The Germans' band is asked to play less often, a change that Beutle attributes to the new craze for "coon songs. Ragtime" (74).

The anti-German sentiments in Prank are fueled by the outbreak of the First World War in 1914. Two years later, as the United States remains neutral in the war amid widespread public pressure to enter it on the side of the British, Beutle is still stridently pro-German and does not understand why others do not accept his explanation that he is loyal to both Germany and the United States. Loats, however, says, "I don't care if they drop a thousand bombs on the Kaiser's head. I don't feel so German now. My children, they're born here, this is their country. . . . I just want America to stay out of it, this war" (77).

After the United States declares war on Germany in April 1917,

Beutle's protestation that he buys Liberty Bonds and has a son fighting for the United States makes no difference to the gangs who throw a rock through his window, burn his fields, and call him "fucken dirty Dutchman" and "baby raper" (79). Beutle's son dies in the war, and Messermacher's son Karl, who is the telegraph operator in Prank, is badly beaten and barely escapes hanging by a lynch mob that accuses him of sending American secrets to the kaiser in Germany.

Anti-German sentiments continue to run high after the war. Beutle's twin granddaughters are kidnapped and raped by unknown assailants, and the three Germans believe that "the Americans" of Prank have committed the crime as revenge for alleged German atrocities in Belgium during the war. By 1920 the three families never go to Prank, instead traveling to a town thirty miles away, where there are more Germans than Irish. Beutle rarely plays his accordion. The time when the three Germans and their music stood at the center of Prank social life is gone forever. The joke of the town's name turns out to be the irony that its founders are no longer welcome there.

Karl Messermacher, who went to Chicago after his run in with the lynch mob, comes home in 1923 driving a new automobile and joking that the mob did him a favor. In Chicago the telegraph company promoted him to an executive position, and he has changed his name to Charlie Sharp. Like Silvano/Bob Joe, he is intent on being "American," and he dismisses accordion music as "old-country junk" (84). As hatred of Germans becomes overshadowed by new hysterias about Communists, Jews, and Catholics, the other children become reinvolved in Prank social life. Some marry "Americans," and one of Messermacher's daughters marries an Irish American.

ACCORDION CRIMES

In 1924 Messermacher, the richest of the three Germans announces that he is moving to Texas to grow cotton and changing his name to Sharp, because Charlie's life has been easier since he took an "American" name. The green accordion goes to Texas with him. In the spring of 1929 Messermacher dies and leaves Beutle two thousand dollars worth of radio stock, which is increasing in value rapidly.

Beutle spends some of the new wealth on one last sexual folly. Unhappy about his decreasing sexual prowess, he takes the train to Topeka, Kansas, where a quack who calls himself Dr. Squam implants pieces of goat gland in Beutle's scrotum. By the end of the long train ride back home the next day, he has developed gangrene. He dies thinking "at least there was German accordion music where he was going" (89). Obsessed by sex and his "German superiority," Beutle has become a seriocomic grotesque, a man totally absorbed in his beliefs and passions.

After Beutle's death his son Percy Claude tells Charlie Sharp to sell the radio stock, but Charlie delays the sale, losing the Beutles' fortune and his own in the stock market crash of 1929. He shoots himself in the face but does not die, and he spends the rest of his life being fed through a funnel in a dim room of the family ranch in Texas. Percy Claude sells the farm to a couple whose bank fails before he can cash their check. He ends up working for the Civilian Conservation Corps during the Depression. As Proulx informs the reader in a flash-forward, however, Percy Claude's son Rawley later "pieced together his grandfather's farm and more" (91), grew wealthy, gave money to start the Prank Farm Pioneer Museum to honor the three Germans' achievement, and hired private investigators to look for his grandfather's green accordion. They are still searching in 1985, when Rawley meets his death in a classic Proulx twist of fate.

While visiting Yellowstone National Park, Rawley slips on a roll of film he has dropped, falls into a hot spring, and climbs out blinded and knowing he is near death, "only to fall into another hotter pool" (91).

This second section of the novel emphasizes the lesson of Frank Archivi's death in part 1: wealth and social prominence are not protection against chance events and the forces of history. At the same time, however, it emphasizes how hatred and prejudice continue because people choose to express them and allow them to motivate actions that mushroom out of control. Another irony is Beutle's grandson's search for the cultural heritage that his parents' generation cast aside, a search that is repeated by others as the novel moves into the second half of the twentieth century.

"Spider, Bite Me"

The next owner of the little green accordion is Abelardo Relámpago Salazar, who buys it for five dollars in 1924 in a Texas barbershop. The Relámpagos have been American citizens since the United States bought the strip of land north of the Rio Grande from Texas in 1848, but Anglo Texans still disparage them as Mexicans. They are *Tejanos* (Texans of Mexican descent), and over the years their culture has evolved through contact with other ethnic groups, as well as absence from their ancestral roots. Abelardo's wife, Adina, has seen evidence of this evolution firsthand. During her childhood, her family's visits to relatives in Mexico grew less frequent as relatives there "commented unpleasantly about the Texas children's debased Spanish and impolite ways; they held an image of these little *norteños* running as mongrel dog packs up in *Tejas*" (107).

Although he bears the family name, Abelardo is not in a strict sense a Relámpago. He was abandoned by his mother as an infant and taken in by the Relámpagos, a poor but proud family that for generations has owned an adobe house and a little land by the river in Boogie, Texas. Because he survives all the biological offspring of the Relámpagos, however, he inherits the property and lives there with his wife and family until 1936. Then an Anglo Texan cotton grower decides he needs the land and contrives to prove that he owns it, paying Abelardo fifty dollars not to dispute the claim.

As a man with no past, Abelardo invents one, yet another of the self-definers in the novel. Romanticizing the house he has lost as an ancient birthright now gone, he wakes up every morning "expecting the smell of the river, and from beyond it the imagined perfume of that beautiful and tragic country where perhaps he was born" (100). He also creates a romantic role for himself in the present. A busboy in a small café during the day, he enters the "other world" of his music at night, earning respect as a performer from the same people who look down on him in the restaurant. Abelardo forges a new heritage for himself through his music. While the accordion maker and the Germans play the music of their homelands, Abelardo is one of a group of musicians who are creating their own *tejano* musical style. As the music scholar Manuel H. Peña explains, in the mid-1920s a distinctive *tejano* musical style began to emerge from the *norteño* (northern) music of the region of Mexico just south of the border, sparked by the interest of major American record companies in tapping into the Mexican American market in the southwestern United States. Like the real-life musicians he mentions as his friends, Abelardo makes hundreds of recordings during the 1930s, singing in Spanish for about ten dollars a session. During the war, the scarcity of record-making materials dried up this outlet for *tejano* music. After the war the major American companies turned their attention almost exclusively to mainstream popular music.[5]

The music that became known as *conjunto* (ensemble) emerged during the Second World War, beginning as a group anchored by at least one diatonic button accordion and usually including a bajo sexto, a twelve-string Mexican guitar. As Abelardo explains to one of his sons in 1950, "I learned to play in the fields, from Narcisco. Narcisco Martínez, *el Huracán del Valle,* started it, started the *conjunto* music. . . . and pretty soon, after the war, there were four or five good *conjuntos*—me, Narcisco, Pedro Ayala, José Rodríguez, Santiago Jiménez, Jesús Casiano" (125).

Conjunto is Abelardo's true heritage, authentic music played by poor people for their working-class compatriots. As "*Tejanos* carried it through the cotton fields, all over the country, up in the beet fields, Oregon and wherever," the music grew popular, and Abelardo and other *conjuntos* began following the "taco circuit," playing for the field workers' Saturday night dances while working at other jobs during the week (125).

Abelardo's wife, Adina, considers herself a realist. When they lose their house in Boogie, the family heads for San Antonio, but gets only as far as Hornet, six miles away, before their truck breaks down. Adina rents a trailer on the edge of the barrio and moves the family into it. She hates the old house and the heritage it represents to her husband, and she is pleased that the new place, though worn, is bigger than the old house and has indoor plumbing instead of an outhouse.

She urges her children to "talk American" at home as well as at school, and gives all but the eldest, Crescencio, "American" names—

Baby, Chris, and Betty. Abelardo insists that they also have Mexican names, to which Adina responds angrily that he might as well give them Indian names and "put them as low as you can get!" (106). Abelardo complains to Baby years later that Adina wants him to be "an ass-licking Anglo doughball" (125). As a result of this fundamental disagreement, the youngest child is called Betty by her mother and Félida by her father.

Adina is ironically the member of the family who knows about her roots in Mexico, but she ended contact with her relatives there after her marriage and says they mean nothing to her because she and her children are Americans. Yet her "deep past was caught unconsciously in her cooking" (107). After moving to Hornet, she also turns her back on the old religion, adopting the beliefs of two Yahweh's Wonder missionaries named Darren and Clarice Leak, a blond Anglo husband and wife who visit Adina's home and eat her food while their children wait in their hot car, forbidden to play with the Relámpago children. Abelardo recognizes the Leaks' hypocrisy and considers them "stupid, fanatic and dangerous" (116), but Adina refuses to listen to him.

Feeling herself caught between the old world of Mexico and the new world of the Anglo Texans, Adina tells her children that the way to success is a good "American" education. In the segregated school system of Hornet all the teachers at the "Mexican" school are Anglos, mostly new teachers from the North dedicated to the melting-pot ideal of American education. Like immigrant and minority students elsewhere, students are expected to speak English and conform to the standards of the dominant American culture. In Hornet they are fined a penny every time they use a Spanish word, an expensive mistake in the Depression era. When Baby and Chris bring their accordions to school and play a song written by their father, their teacher, from Chicago, calls the accordion "a rather *stupid* instrument," and adds, "Polacks play it" (114). The children do not know what a polack is and come to the conclusion it must be a polar bear—a humorous example of how prejudice is learned, not innate.

The teachers also inflict demeaning punishments for minor misdemeanors. After one particularly humiliating punishment, Crescencio, known as Chencho, drops out of school. He is drafted into the army as soon as he turns eighteen, in 1943. The army assigns him to a Mexican American squad that is sent to the Solomon Islands, where only a few survive the bloody fighting. Chencho is killed—ironically, not in battle. While he is jitterbugging with another soldier, he kicks a cinder block wall, and it falls on him.

Baby and Chris, like their father, live through their music. Yet, despite their musical gifts, the brothers never make it big, partly through the racism and lack of interest in ethnic music that was widespread in the mainstream recording business in the 1940s and early 1950s, and partly through the kind of unpredictable bad luck that strikes characters throughout the novel. As boys they win a talent contest with a prize of two hundred dollars and a guest appearance on a powerful radio station, but shortly before they are to perform a strong wind blows down the radio tower, knocking the station off the air.

Abelardo has a reason to treasure his little green accordion aside from the music he plays on it. At some point in the late 1930s or early 1940s, a man who is probably a drug dealer comes into the café and offers him an "opportunity." Once a month the man will leave a package on an empty chair at his table, and Abelardo, with no questions asked, will carry it out the back door and place it in an empty car. In return the man will leave a thousand-dollar bill beneath his plate for Abelardo. Abelardo earns fourteen of these bills before the man stops coming to the café. Such a large amount of money seems "abstract" to Abelardo. "So large a bill could not be real money," he thinks, so he glues the bills inside the bellows of his green accordion (119). Now the green accordion, a symbol of treasured ethnic traditions lost in the American melting pot, has a literal treasure hidden within it, reinforcing the irony of its unrecognized value. At the same time the source of the money is tainted, like the foundations of fortunes made later in the novel.

After the Second World War, as *conjunto* continues to evolve, some old timers complain that Baby and Chris play too fast. During this period trap drums and chromatic accordions were added to many ensembles, and the style of the music began to change. The brothers are part of *la nueva generacíon* (the new generation), which according to Peña refined and consolidated the *conjunto* style between 1945 and 1960.

In 1946 Abelardo discovers to his surprise that fourteen-year-old Félida/Betty is perhaps the most musically talented of the children. Believing that girls should not be musicians, he has never encouraged her as he has the boys, so he is amazed one morning to hear her playing "[c]elestial music" on the green accordion, which he alone is allowed to touch, and singing in a "melting" tone like none he has heard before (95). Angry that his daughter should have more talent than her brothers, he tells her never to touch his green accordion again. (Women in *conjunto* bands were, in fact, rare.) Hurt by her father's anger, she confides her dream of becoming a musician to an Anglo teacher, who invites her to his house to play for him. But before she can even take the green accordion from its case, he rapes her. When she arrives home, her father is enraged that she has taken his accordion, and during the night the doubly betrayed girl runs away, leaving a knife stuck in the bellows of the accordion.

In the early 1950s Baby and Chris continue to play *conjunto*. Many of their generation prefer big-band music or "the strange hybrid fusion of jazz, rumba and swing," but they still find an audience for their music, especially among Korean War veterans, some of them college students. "They listen," Chris explains, "not because we're good, though we are good, but because we are theirs" (127). Baby and Chris are discovering the beginning of the folk music craze of the late 1950s and early 1960s, a search for roots by the children of those first-generation Americans who cast aside their cultural heritage to become the kind of "Americans" that the Relámpago children's teachers have trained them to be.

In 1952 Chris, who has been in and out of trouble with the law, surprises everyone by joining the Yahweh's Wonders and marrying the Leaks' daughter Lorraine. Her parents, "caught in the trap of their own preaching about brotherhood" (128), attend the wedding but stay away from the fiesta that Abelardo and Adina give for the couple, enraging Abelardo with their hypocritical superiority. Saying he will play only religious music now, Chris stops playing with Baby at clubs and dances.

Baby marries Rita Sánchez, a teacher and community activist, who believes in his musical talent. Yet, when Rita suggests that he could be famous, he responds, "Yeah? And change my name, Like Andrés Rábago to Andy Russell? And Danny Flores to Chuck Rio? Like Richard Valenzuela to Ritchie Valens? Na, na, na" (130–31).

Although he has played other music to pick up extra money and has disagreed with his father about their music in the past, Baby now embraces the music that his father has passed on to him: "Now Baby understood his father's greatness without jealousy or envy. Saw his inventiveness, his place in the history of music. When they sang together now, he felt his voice embrace that of his father, a kind of sexless marrying like two streams of water coming together. Together they were in a closeness not even lovers could know, as the shadows of two birds at different altitudes cross the ground touching." Audiences recognize their affinity, "smothering them in admiration" (131), but despite their closeness Abalardo never lets Baby play the green accordion.

Baby inherits Abelardo's accordion, however, after Abelardo is bitten several times by a poisonous brown recluse spider and dies, largely because of the inadequate medical treatment available to the poor. He dies playing the green accordion. Hundreds of people attend his funeral, where Baby plays every song his father has ever written.

Soon after Abelardo's death the family discovers how Chris can afford to own an expensive camper van on a cab driver's salary. Chris is stopped at the border coming back from Mexico with his wife and children, and drugs are discovered hidden in the propane tanks. As Chris's trial is about to begin, Darren Leak, bursts into the courtroom with Chris's revolver and takes revenge. Calling Chris a "dirty Mexican nigger" who "mixed your dirty bloody with ours" (136), the "man of God" kills Chris and himself, revealing the truth behind his lifetime of preaching brotherly love.

Baby, who becomes well known in the Southwest as Baby Lightning, makes more than twenty records, and has played as far away as Canada, Chicago, and New York (actually Albany). Though his music has evolved, he remains true to his father's *conjunto* roots and uses the green accordion to play some of his father's music. In 1955, after a concert in Minneapolis, he meets his sister, whom he has not seen since she left home at fourteen. Now definitely Betty, she has married Tony, an Italian bandleader, and plays the piano accordion on the club date circuit with his band. A talented musician, she can "cover standards and Latin and ethnic and pop, yes, and swing and hot jazz, even hillbilly and semiclassical" (142). She is "good at the ethnic stuff" (139) popular at weddings and anniversary parties—such as Italian, Greek, Jewish, Polish, Hungarian, and Swedish music—every kind of music but that of her own people, which she denigrates. She tells Baby he is "stuck," still playing "what our father played, or at least what you and Chris played years and years ago, just the same stuff, the old *conjunto*" (140) and says he should play Latin jazz. She calls the diatonic accordion "the instrument of unsuccessful men, of poor immigrants and failures" and "a nasty toy for amateurs and drunks" (142). Having extended her anger at her father's male chauvinism to his music, she asserts that she is "not stuck with *conjunto*" like her brother. The argument continues until Baby, who sees that they will never come to any agreement, leaves. As he walks into his hotel with tears in his eyes, he realizes that in his grief he has forgotten the green accordion in the taxi cab. He makes many telephone calls but can never find it.

Though Baby carries on his father's music, an important part of his heritage is lost with the green accordion—along with the fourteen thousand dollars still hidden in its bellows. The final words of the section are Betty's. After her husband refers to the recently departed Baby as a "yo-yo," she bursts into tears. When Tony tries to comfort her, she pushes him away and thinks: "An Italian!" (143). Like Bob Joe and Charlie Sharp, Betty has redefined herself as an "American" with no particular roots. In her case, as in many others, "Americanization" does not foster tolerance.

"Hitchhiking in a Wheelchair"

The next owner of the accordion is Dolor Gagnon, who is in Minneapolis by chance because he took the wrong plane on his way home to be discharged from the army. Having been placed in an orphanage by his mother when he was two, he, like Abelardo before him, has no past and is about to set out in search of his roots.

Dolor is the rootless son of a rootless son. His father, Charles Gagnon, was an orphan who stayed alive by playing a harmonica and later a little one-row button accordion for pennies in the streets of Paris. Later he graduated to playing in rough *bals musette* (dance halls). By the 1920s he had discovered jazz, bought a better accordion, and become convinced that only luck and connections made other jazz accordionists famous while he labored in obscurity.

Then he found himself in trouble. Having impregnated two women, he got involved in a brawl with the male relatives of the women, each of whom expected him to marry her. During the fight, discarded cigarettes started a fire. Both women were killed in the blaze, but Charles escaped, as did one woman's father, who vowed revenge.

Thus, in 1931 Charles fled Paris, worked his way across the Atlantic, and ended up in Quebec, where in less than a year he married a woman named Delphine and fathered a child. Any kind of work was hard to find during the Great Depression, and he was not inclined to seek work as a musician because "he disdained the drawling, mangled language and the Québécois musette style, . . . and he despised the stupid reels and *gigues* [jigs] of the carrot farmer and *bûcheron* [lumberman]" (150). While it shares French roots with the music Charles played in Paris dance halls (which he also disliked), this Québécois music, like Abelardo's, evolved into the distinct expression of a particular ethnic group influenced by a particular environment.

Finally Delphine's brother found him a job at a box mill in Random, Maine, where Charles and Delphine rented a shack without electricity or plumbing. Blaming Delphine for not telling him before their marriage that she was part Abenaki, Charles claimed that he was "tricked and trapped by wily redskins," first into his "unsavory marriage" to a "half-breed" and later into moving to the "brutally provincial cul-de-sac" of northern Maine (153). Delphine despised the even-worse-off "dirty Irish" family who live in a shack near the dump—yet another example in the novel of how prejudice breeds more prejudice.

In the spring of 1937 Charles lost all four fingers of his right hand in an accident at the mill, and by the end of the year he had deserted his wife and six children. The only memento of him is a charred accordion that Delphine rescued from the woodstove, where Charles threw it after trying unsuccessfully to play it with only one good hand. Delphine's brother, who had moved to Providence, sends bus fare for her and the two oldest children, who were old enough to work.

The other children, including two-year-old Dolor, were sent to Birdnest, an old house converted into an orphanage, where Dolor grows up without any contact with his siblings. The director of the orphanage makes him take "a regular boy's name" (158), Frank, but he drops it as soon as he turns eighteen, graduates from high school, and leaves the orphanage. On the day of his departure, the director gives him a package that came with him when he arrived; it contains the charred accordion. His only legacy is his father's accordion, which, he soon learns, is damaged beyond repair.

Dolor enlists in the army, but after a year a mysterious illness leaves him partially paralyzed for a time and earns him a medical discharge. When he returns to Random in search of his roots, he discovers that no one there remembers his parents, and he is "a stranger in his hometown" (166). Dolor himself knows so little about his family and his heritage that he does not realize, until Emma—the wife of his rediscovered acquaintance Wilf Ballou—tells him, that his name is a variation of *douleur,* the French word for "pain." When Emma says it is "funny" that he is French but cannot speak it, he thinks "how funny it was, his name taken from him, the language lost, his religion changed, the past unknown, the person he had been for the first two years of his life erased." He fantasizes that someday "he would wake speaking and thinking in French, a joyous man with many friends, his lost family would come back" (173). Dolor sometimes imagines himself speaking French, but—daydreams aside— he never learns the language, nor does he overcome the chronic depression that seems to deepen the longer he stays in Random.

He invents a family history to go with his father's burned accordion, claiming that his father died while saving his children from the fire that damaged his accordion. Wilf, another former inmate of the orphanage, says this fiction sounds like every other orphan's tale of how he ended up at Birdnest.

Wilf, who plays the fiddle, and Dolor, who is gradually learning to play the green accordion, begin playing together. Their first gig is a comic scene: a surprise birthday party for an unwilling wife, where Dolor and Wilf's first attempt at using a secondhand set of electric amplifiers nearly electrocutes the guest of honor and almost burns down the house.

Dolor is unhappy with the music they are playing, pop tunes and popular folk songs such as "Michael Row the Boat Ashore" and "Tom Dooley"—music from a tradition that is not his—but he is unsure what his tradition is. Emma, whose father used to play "Frenchie" music, says her father has switched to hillbilly music and used his old records of traditional French Canadian music for target practice. Dolor finally drives to Montmagny, Quebec, where he hears some of the best performers of the old regional music playing as he imagines his father must have played. The irony of course is that while this music is the heritage of his mother's family, his father the musician despised it.

Dolor later remembers his experience in Montmagny as "the greatest night in his life, the one he later pulled up from submerged dreams, though the memory was flawed by a phantasm assumption. He believed that on that evening he had understood and spoken French" (183). Yet, driving back to Random, he has different thoughts. Though the music he has heard is his "by blood inheritance," he "could not learn it because he didn't speak French, because he lived in a place where the music was no longed admired or played" (184). As Emma's sister tells him later, everybody in Random is "caught between being French and being American" (195).

During this time Dolor has also been falling in love with Emma, in part, he thinks, because "he wanted Wilf's life" but "most deeply because she was French . . . and because of her dozens of relatives . . . , the complex interconnections of blood extending up over the border and to the St. Lawrence south shore and down through New England and into the south" (176).

Such thoughts and the passing fancy that he could marry Emma if Wilf should die seem to be the triggers for a renewal of the leg pain he experienced in the army. After Wilf dies a horrible death in a truck accident, Dolor wakes up one morning to discover that he cannot move his legs at all. The doctors at the V.A. hospital can find no cause for his paralysis, which seems to be related to Dolor's guilty thought that wishing his friend dead may have made it so. He becomes a virtual prisoner in his rented room. His only way into town is by hitchhiking, and since only pick-up trucks have room for his cumbersome wheelchair and since getting him in and out requires time and energy, rides are hard to find.

Emma comes to his rescue, not to marry him—she is engaged to someone else—but to drag him off to a cousin's wedding, on the pretense that her father and fiancé will play some of the old music. They do play two songs, badly, before switching to country-and-western music. The real reason for bringing Dolor to the wedding seems to be hooking him up with Emma's sister Anne-Marie, who calls herself Mitzi and addresses Dolor as Frank.

Anne-Marie/Mitzi takes Dolor to a shrine of St. Jude at the comically improbable location of Lake Picklecake, where she is sure his paralysis will be cured. Indeed, as Dolor pins a votive medal to the shrine he is moved by "[s]ome unknown sensation—was it faith?"—and believes he has "heard a holy voice" (193). When they get to the motel where they are staying, Dolor gets out of the car and walks. Though he and Mitzi believe his recovery is a miracle, the skeptical reader may see it as a case of psychosomatic illness cured by powerful suggestion.

Dolor and Mitzi are married a month later. At her cousin's wedding Dolor met her father's sister, Delphine Barbeau, who has expressed an interest in him after hearing his last name. At his wedding Delphine, who is near death from cancer, tells him, "Now you married your cousin. You fool." When he says he has no cousins and asks what she means, she says accusingly, "Wife, . . . you married your wife" (194). Before he can ask her to explain she has a fit of coughing and has to be carried out. She dies soon after, and Dolor never learns what the reader surmises: Delphine is his mother, and he has always been a part of that vast network of family that has made Emma so desirable to him.

Mitzi's solution to the problem with Random—that everyone is "caught between being French and being American" (195)—is not to search for their roots but to become more "American." She asks Dolor to change his name to the "American"-sounding Frank Gaines, just as she has opted for the "American" name Mitzi, which is actually the German diminutive for "Maria." Dolor agrees to be Frank, but he insists on keeping his last name. Mitzi wants to leave Ransom and be "American" in Portland or Boston because she is tired of the "here's-another-Frenchie look" she gets in local stores. Since the accordion is "sort of a instrument they make fun of, a Frenchie thing" (196), she hopes he will let Emma and her new husband sell it for him while they are on their honeymoon in Louisiana, where they should be able to get a good price.

Dolor thinks that none of these things matter, and agrees to the plan to sell the accordion. He is "limp with happiness" during these early days of marriage (195). Yet "already the red idea was simmering that such intoxicating sweetness of life couldn't last" (195). He fears that his depression and paralysis will return, and while Emma and her husband, Emil, are on their way to Louisiana, he commits suicide, leaving a note that reads "I am happy" (198). In the next section of the novel the reader learns that he has decapitated himself with a chainsaw.

Of all the seekers after self-definition in *Accordion Crimes,* Dolor is perhaps the saddest. Having been robbed of his roots as a child, he never finds the sense of community that the equally root-less Abelardo not only inherits but builds on to create his own her-itage. More so than anyone else in the appropriately named town of Random, he is caught between two cultures and at home in neither. Finally, feeling convinced that he owns nothing but his depression, he becomes a grotesque embodiment of his overwhelming sadness.

"Don't Let a Dead Man Shake You by the Hand"

The next owner of the green accordion is Buddy Malefoot, a Louisiana Cajun who has paid $115 for it, probably more than he had to, because he felt sorry for Dolor's widow. Buddy's last name is suggestive because he has recently hurt his foot working on an oil rig, but the name Malefoot seems to have a different connotation— at least to their enemies, who say it "derived from *malfrat,* or gang-ster" (203). Having come from France in the seventeenth century, the Malefoots are "a tangled clan of nodes and connecting rhizomes that spread over the continent like the fila of a great fungus" (203).The family's travels in the New World are typical of the Cajun people, whose name evolved from *Acadian,* the designation given the French colonists of Acadie, which became Nova Scotia when it was ceded to the British in 1713. After the thousands of Acadians refused to swear allegiance to the British crown, the British shipped many to the American colonies while others fled to French colonies elsewhere. The Malefoots wandered back and forth for several decades before ending up in the French colony of Louisiana a few years before it was ceded to Spain in 1763. Then, they and other Acadians

> traveled north and west into the hot, dripping, watery country of the Opelousas, Attakaps, Chitimachas, Houmas, to the Acadian coasts, the bayous Têche and Courtableau, learning to pole fragile bateaux and live in the humid damp. They mixed and mingled, blended and combined their blood with that of the local tribes, Haitians, West Indians, slaves, Germans, Spanish, Free People of Color . . . , *nègres libres* and Anglo settlers, even *américains,* shaping mélo-mélo culture steeped in French, and the accordion, borrowed from the Germans, livelied the kitchen music of the prairie parishes, the fiddle had its way in the watery parishes. (203–4)

Until recently the Malefoots and their neighbors have practiced a way of life that has remained essentially unchanged for centuries. Yet, as Buddy's father, Onesiphore, points out, attitudes and lifestyles have begun to change in his son's generation. He blames compulsory education at schools where they "talk only *américain*" for the lack of respect that the young show toward their elders and for their preference for "supermarket food" over "homegrown food" cooked in traditional Cajun dishes. He complains that his children spoke "perfect French" before being inundated with "American" culture at school (202). Government authorization of offshore oil drilling in 1953 has also had a major influence on the Cajun lifestyle. Buddy calls French a "secret language [that] don't work" (202) and says it is useless to him on the oil rig, where many of the men come from Texas and Oklahoma. Buddy's Cajun accordion music is as unwelcome among these men as his French.

Furthermore, modern efforts to control the flooding of the Mississippi are altering the Cajuns' landscape and hurting one of their traditional livelihoods. The shrimp beds are dying because the U.S. Army Corps of Engineers has built levees, "cutting off the rich silt deposits that had traveled all the way from the heartland of the continent and that had fed the great marshes forever. . . . The swamps and marshes were dissolving, sinking, shrinking away" (204). A flash-forward explains that within a generation five hundred square miles of swampland has been washed away. Other marshes have been turned into freshwater rice paddies or drained for pasture land, thus altering the livelihoods of men who for generations have "dragged for shrimp, tonged oysters, fished" (204). When the state began paving the old dirt roads in the 1930s, it set in motion another change. By 1959 people were no longer building their houses along waterways and traveling by pirogue. Their houses were along roadways, and they traveled by motor vehicle.

Yet, in 1959, the year in which Buddy buys the green accordion, the Cajun culture is still so remarkably intact that national magazines, responding to the new craze for folk culture, are sending photographers and writers to cover the Cajuns' way of life, and the area is beginning to attract tourists. Onesiphore calls a new restaurant built by a Texan "a place for tourists come to see the Cajuns, like monkeys" and suggests putting up a sign that says *"CAJUN-LAND"* (208).

The intersection of one outsider, a photographer, with Cajun culture is the subject of one of the most humorous episodes in the novel, and it introduces two memorable grotesques. Like much of Proulx's humor, however, the comedy is rooted in pain.

The episode begins when Buddy's otherwise "modern" wife goes to Mrs. Blush Leleur, a *traîteuse* or healer, for help in curing her mother-in-law's coldheartedness, which began years ago when Buddy's sister, Belle, was killed by a drive-by shooter who mistook her for someone else in the dark. Ever since then Mme Malefoot has shown no affection to any living being except her yellow cat, and she has been obsessively painting portraits of her dead daughter. The best of her efforts is enshrined in her daughter's old bedroom, "framed in a black-enamel toilet seat with gilded margin, the lid hiding the portrait unless it was lifted" (210).

The *traîteuse* explains to the daughter-in-law that if the cat dies, Mme Malefoot's "affection will take flight and fasten to the first one who approaches her with consoling words" (216). Mrs. Leleur's prediction sets in motion a successful plot to kidnap the wily and cautious cat and send him to a cruel death as bait in the Saturday night dogfights. Unfortunately for the daughter-in-law and her family, the first person Mme Malefoot sees is Olga Buckle, a photographer who has been taking pictures of events such as "illegal cockfights, flashlight alligator hunts, horses being fixed with charms and potions to win or lose races, miscegenation, arm wrestling matches where the winner snaps the loser's ulna, staring matches, bad-blood ambushes, shooting victims, raped and disheveled girls telling their stories, raids on stills, swamp hideouts with escaped convicts in residence, or . . . dogfights to the death" (217–18). Like Walter Welter, the photographer in "Negatives," this voyeur into the foibles, vices, and depravities of others gives no thought to her subjects' possible reactions to her photographs, nor does she sense personal danger. Using her camera as a "shield against involvement," she considers "her position to be one of privilege and safety, for she had an important reputation, came from the north, and *she knew better*" (218).

Driving home from the dogfights, Olga stops to photograph the weeping Mme Malefoot in her night gown and dirty slippers just as she has finished digging a grave for her dead cat. Though Olga is taller than Belle, she has similar curly blonde hair, and as the delusional Mme Malefoot looks up through teary eyes, Olga "seemed to her to be the angel of Belle come to console her mother." Convincing herself that Belle is wearing an "ugly carnival mask" so that others will not know she has returned from the dead, the old woman pulls Olga, who continues snapping photographs, into the house and lavishes her with attention and affection (219). After the photographer becomes uncomfortable and leaves, Mme Malefoot—holding firmly to her delusion to the last—concludes, "The angels were calling her child back to heaven" (220).

While Mme Malefoot's grief-motivated delusions and obsessions make her a grotesque character, Olga is made grotesque by her ego. Her sense of superiority to her subjects allows her to divorce herself from any feelings for them or anyone else. In a flash-forward, however, the narrator reveals that Olga eventually finds herself in a situation where she cannot use her camera as a "shield." Stopped at a red light, she is shot in the left eye by a nine-year-old firing from an apartment window. The shooting makes her a "celebrity victim" and ironically brings attention and acclaim to her work.

Onesiphore and Buddy both like the sound of the green accordion and play it at a dance, but when Octave, a black neighbor, offers to buy it for $250, Buddy and Onesiphore agree to sell it. Octave wants the green accordion not only because he likes the way it sounds and is sure he could play it better than either Malefoot but mainly because while he was listening to Onesiphore play it, Octave saw his own eyes reflected in its surface and felt that "it had looked him in the eye," that it is "powerfully alive" (226).

Octave's story is in many ways representative of the African American experience. He is the great-great-grandson of an African brought to the Mississippi Delta as a slave, a gifted metal smith, whose son, Cordozar, escaped to Canada, leaving behind his family, and fought in the Union Army during the Civil War. After the war he was one of many black men who joined the U.S. Cavalry, fighting and dying in the West during the Indian Wars. Zephyr, the child Cordozar left behind, was a sharecropper in Vanilla, Mississippi, and a banjo player who spent a few years playing the banjo in a carnival show touring the West, until the show folded in Nevada, forcing him to return to Vanilla, where like most sharecroppers, he is "cheated annually of the money he earned" by the white man who owns the land (237).

After Zephyr dies, in May 1955, his daughter, Lamb, moves to Bayou Féroce, Louisiana, with her boyfriend and her three children, Octave and his two sisters. A year later the boyfriend, Warfield Dunks, suffers one of the humorously ironic, random deaths that are sprinkled throughout the novel: "[H]e stopped to watch a six-hundred-pound wild boar running down the midline of the highway and a Chevrolet driven by an elderly white woman struck him from behind" (239). Lamb supports her children by working as a domestic, and Octave becomes a fisherman in the Gulf, saving money for a train ticket to Chicago, where he plans to make it big as a musician.

Octave plays zydeco, a blend of Creole, Cajun, and Caribbean influences with blues and rhythm and blues, which emerged in Louisiana just after the Second World War. After buying the green accordion, he takes it to a club in Houston, where he expects to alternate sets with Clifton, a musician who plays a piano accordion. Clifton has car trouble, however, and Octave plays all night. Proulx's description of his performance captures the flavor of his music: "He started hot and hard, held the accordion over his head for a triple bellows shake, rotating the corners of the bellows in a semi-circular twist, rolled out like a plane flying acrobatics into diatonic clusters using every inch of the long bellows and shifting its action skillfully, swooping and diving into a rocking palm section that had the dance floor jammed tight in three minutes" (230). Later he plays "'Don't Let a Dead Man Shake Your Hand,' buttons clicking, the bellows sucking in breath and jetting it out in puffs, distorting the tones by swinging the accordion over his head, slamming into swells and then choking it down, scratching and rubbing and rattling the backs of his fingernails along the ridges of the bellows" (232).

Thirty-five years later someone who was in the club still remembers "the night Octave tore off the roof with that green two-row," and says Octave never played as well again (232). Some of the people in the club, however, keep calling for Clifton, and Octave concludes that he should not have bought the green accordion. He decides to sell it in Chicago and buy a piano accordion like Clifton's. He does not realize at the time that his performance is "the single burning night that comes at the top of a life, and it's all downhill from there, no matter what happens" (232).

At this point in the novel, the green accordion ceases to be central to its owners' lives. When Octave arrives in Chicago in 1960, the strap on the accordion case breaks in the train station and the accordion falls out and is damaged. Now it makes "a sound like what a human being would make if it got turned into an instrument. . . . like somebody choking" (235). Octave discovers that no one in Chicago is interested in zydeco; they play "all blues, blues, blues . . . electrified guitar urban blues, loud and fast and gritty" (233), music that fits the hard and fast-paced Chicago lifestyle. The economic boom that lured so many southern blacks to Chicago during and after the Second World War has ended, and over the next few years Octave's fortunes rise and fall with the economy, as he works intermittently in construction and develops a drug habit. He pawns the green accordion and buys a piano accordion on time. He begins to like urban blues, "but he still played zydeco, ashamed because it was southern nigger music" (236)—just as Félida/Betty and children of immigrants in other parts of the novel become embarrassed by their musical heritage.

Octave gets blacklisted in the construction industry, works a long succession of odd jobs, and spends a few years in jail. There he completes junior college, starts reading the *Wall Street Journal* and financial magazines, and comes up with a plan to get rich that utilizes sludge, the solid matter that is precipitated in water and sewage-treatment processes. After he is released in 1978, sixteen banks turn down his loan applications, so he robs a supermarket and uses the money to buy eight acres of land in Louisiana: "By 1990 he owned a five-hundred-acre model landfill and was a major conduit for New York City sludge which went from him to fields in Iowa, the Dakotas, Nebraska, Colorado, Texas and California" (248).

Octave's success is an example of the "rags to riches" American Dream; yet, in Proulx's sardonically humorous telling of the fairy tale that lured so many immigrants to the New World, the "hero" finances his venture through a criminal act and makes his fortune by selling other people's excrement. By analogy, however, Octave's story is not so different from that of the great robber barons, American financiers of the nineteenth century who amassed vast fortunes and created huge monopolies while underpaying their workers and overcharging the American consumer. Octave, at least, sells a product that is useful and ecologically sound. The irony of the way in which he got his start, of course, is that he had fourteen thousand dollars in the green accordion and pawned the instrument without ever knowing its true worth, either for what was hidden in it or for the heritage it represents. After he becomes rich, Octave gives up accordion playing and does not even like to listen to accordion music, becoming yet another Proulx character who renounces his ethnic identity in an attempt to become a part of the American melting pot.

This section of the novel also follows the fortunes of Octave's sister Ida, who is "six foot two and almost three hundred pounds at eighteen, homely and dark black, with a big potato nose and gap teeth." When she was in the eighth grade, Ida and her friend Tamonette, who "shared a dangerous humor," pulled off the successful prank of surreptitiously pulling white women's hair in a local department store, managing not even to smile at the surprise and consternation they caused until they were safely away from the scene (239). At eighteen in 1960, the year Octave leaves for Chicago, Ida gets involved in the nascent civil rights movement. During her first sit-in at a Woolworth's lunch counter in a nearby town, she disobeys the leader's instruction to practice passive resistance and fights back, suffering a horrible beating as a result. Over the next year she transforms "every sit-in into a riot," until her group leader finally tells her, "You got too much top anger, sister," and sends her home to "figure out a different kind of a way to help your brothers and sisters" (246).

Ida, who has been talking to little old ladies and mystifying her mother by writing in notebooks for years, gathers up her books and papers and moves to Philadelphia, where, surprisingly, she settles into a quiet life. She spends the next thirty years working for a company that prepares and packages airline food, while driving south on weekends to interview still more gray-haired women. Years later she reflects on the civil rights movement and concludes that while it may have done "something fine" in securing civil rights and voting rights legislation, the movement did not do enough to improve the lot of most African Americans: "Seemed like some had got money and power, but they'd left the others behind, curling like shrimps in the smoking fry pans of cities where bodies of children were discovered in trash compactors, blood dripped through ceilings onto somebody's plate at dinner, babies got shot in cross fire, and the names of cities meant something deep bad, unfixable and wrong. Money was rolling in deep waves but not even the foam touched the black shore" (247). Ida, it is finally revealed, has been involved in a lifelong project to collect and record the memories of black women, and her apartment is filled with thousands of their firsthand accounts of their lives and their culture. Channeling her anger at racial injustice into her project, Ida has collected these women's stories from "used-book shops, church bazaars, yard sales, dim, dusty boxes in thrift stores, trash cans and Dumpsters" and by "asking everyone she met, you got any books of letters or whatnot about black women, any black women, everywoman?" (247). Probably the only truly unselfish and genuinely noble character in the novel, Ida is like Quoyle in *The Shipping News* to the extent that she is a physically grotesque character who becomes metaphorically beautiful through her efforts to understand and come to terms with her past. She has no illusions, though, that her heroic efforts to rescue a dying culture from obscurity can make a real difference in the lives of poor black people: "All those notebooks wouldn't save a single one from the hot pan, all those histories of black women, those invisible suffering ones at the bottom of the bag" (247).

As the novel progresses, Americans seem more and more lost and rootless, with no connection to the past and drifting aimlessly in the present. Thinking about Octave, whom she has not seen in years, Ida muses: "Wasn't that the old evil thing, brother and sisters losing each other? Wasn't it the old, old thing, families torn up like scrap paper, the home place left and lost forever?" (247–48). This same "evil thing" takes place over and over in *Accordion Crimes*.

"Hit Hard and Gone Down"

The green accordion does not appear until fairly late in the sixth section of the novel, which begins with the family history of its next owner, Joey Newcomer, whose father changed his name from Hieronim Przybysz to Harry Newcomer. As African Americans begin

moving into their Polish neighborhood in Chicago after the Second
World War, Hieronim/Harry is among the people who hurl rocks
and obscenities at their new black neighbors, apparently missing the
irony that when he was young, descendants of earlier immigrants
once threw stones at him while "calling him a dirty polack, a dumb
hunky" (252). While her son is uninterested in learning about his
Polish roots, Mrs. Józef Przybysz finds an eager audience in her
grandson Joey.

Józef Przybysz was an educated man, a pharmacist in Poland,
but when he came to the United States, immigration inspectors listed
him as illiterate because he could not read or speak English. Working at first in the Chicago stockyards for seventeen cents an hour,
Józef did not make enough money to support his wife and six children and became embittered. He asserted his superiority over the
"dirty" Americans above him on the social ladder while looking
down on other Poles as well, calling them "peasants and fools . . .
stupid as boot heels. . . . They could not even speak Polish well,
nothing, not Russian or German. The poor things had no place, no
language of their own" (260). He hated the Americans' tendency to
lump all central Europeans together as "dumb hunkies," but of
course he was also guilty of ethnic stereotyping.

Józef played the accordion to earn extra money, never playing
for pleasure after he began to do so for pay, as though his music
were somehow demeaned by his having accepted money for it. Yet
he enjoyed a sense of power and superiority over his audience. As
he explained to his wife, the foreman might call him "dumb hunky"
and "stupid polack" at work, but when he played the accordion he
got a form of revenge: "[I]f the foreman is there in the place, maybe
with his disgusting fellow bosses and repulsive wife, he gets up and

dances to my tunes and I make them hot to watch him sweat and twirl" (263). In 1926 Józef started a polka band, picking "an American name, the Polkalookas" and eschewing "old-fashioned" polka music, for something "a little faster and louder" to attract an Americanized ethnic audience. He even formed the popular Baby Polka Band with six-year-old Hieronim and five or six other little children. However, his success in music did not make Józef happy.

Having become a cigar maker, he and hundreds of other cigar rollers traveled all over the country by train, working for a few weeks at a time in cigar shops and "looking for the golden America they had imagined, a place they believed existed somewhere" (265). Józef sent money home at first, but eventually it stopped coming, and his wife was forced to take in boarders, one of whom sodomized Hieronim. When it finally became clear that Józef was not returning, his wife took a job as a cigar maker herself, beginning a period in her life that she looks back on as her "happiest years" (266).

She tells her grandson Joey, "It is not easy to remain yourself, to keep your dignity and place, in a foreign country," offering the example of the boy's grandfather as proof that it is, however, possible. Yet Joey's father derives a different lesson from such stories— "that to be foreign, to be Polish, not to be American, was a terrible thing and all that could be done about it was to change one's name and talk about baseball" (259). Hieronim/Harry also has a different view of the "old bastard" who bullied his children, calling his father "a lousy musician, interested only in the dollar," whose "music was coarse. . . . Crude stuff. The lowest common denominator" (267). He also disputes his father's claim that he was a pharmacist: "I did some checking up and he wasn't nothing but a peasant. Tried to make out he was better over here" (267).

Harry is convinced that the family was happier and better off without his father. After he left, Mrs. Przybysz was reunited with her family, whom Józef shunned because they were "hillbillies" from the Tatra Mountain region, and "Uncle Tic-Tac . . . tried to teach your father the old mountain songs, urged him to write them down in a book to gather these songs from the old generation." After Harry comes back from the Second World War, however, he wants to play what his mother calls "the new kind of polka, 'The Killer Diller Polka,' and one I did not like very much but I've forgotten the name." She regrets that "so much was lost" and hopes that Joey will be able "to save the old Polish music." (267)

In 1967, just before Joey's wedding to Sonia, Harry goes out in his yard barefooted and uses his electric worm probe while standing on the wet grass. He electrocutes himself, becoming yet another character who suffers a comic-ironic death.

Joey seems to have inherited his grandfather's temperament along with his name. He is sullen and short-tempered, quick to blame his misfortunes on others, especially his wife. He also has a tendency to touch the private parts of little girls, including his own daughter. He and Sonia put together a polka act and supplement Joey's meager wages by competing for prize money at contests and festivals. Sonia drinks liniment before each performance because Joey likes the way it gives her voice the "harsh and high . . . sound of ecstasy and raw pain" (322); the liniment, however, contributes to her death from throat cancer in 1985.

Polka festivals have changed over the years. At the first festivals, in the 1960s, where Joey competed before his marriage to Sonia, the organizers "wanted performers to sing in the language or some regional dialect, preferred unusual music and difficult dances."

Those festivals attracted just Polish people at first, but then they "turned into everybody-come, beer-drinking weekend good times" that attracted a crowd not interested in "cultural esoterica" (289). The popularization and commercialization of folk music in the 1960s and 1970s have not preserved the old music, as some might have thought. Instead, the polka, like other forms of ethnic music, has been reduced to its lowest common denominator. Promoters have found it easier and more profitable to simplify and "Americanize" the music rather than to educate audiences about its authentic ethnic forms.

The acts at the 1970 Polish Polka Playoffs demonstrate what has happened to the polka. Novelty acts in goofy costumes, telling jokes about "polacks" and playing pop songs such as "Yes Sir, That's My Baby," are followed by a blind boy who plays religious music. Next a middle-aged woman plays popular songs of the late 1960s, ending "with that good old Polish tune 'Zorba the Greek'" (288). Seeming more ethnic than most of the acts, Joey and Sonia play in a fast style with a "wild honkying minor, a barbarian tension, the feeling of being on the edge of losing control" (284). Sonia's voice seems to say that "this was what it meant to be Polish: misery suppressed, injustices borne, strength in adversity, endurance" (290). Their chief competition is the act that follows theirs, the Bartosik Brothers, who are well known for playing "popular music in *polka* style" and are scheduled to "play a memorial-tribute medley of Jimi Hendrix and Janis Joplin tunes" (291). This act is eliminated, however, when one of the performers shows up drunk and vomits onstage. Joey and Sonia win the contest and the $1500 in prize money. It is not surprising that American polka music has evolved from its roots in Poland. Yet, unlike Abelardo's *conjunto* music, for example, much of the music played at the polka festivals is not the authentic expression of a people's experience. It is no longer ethnic music.

Arriving at the 1970 polka playoffs, with two sick children in a beat-up automobile with a nonfunctioning heater, Joey and Sonia have discovered their accordions are missing from the trunk of their car. When Joey went to a pawnshop to rent substitute piano accordions, he saw the green accordion on an upper shelf and was strangely drawn to it—as other musicians have been before him. Though he does not know how to play a button accordion, Sonia does, and after they win the contest, Joey buys the green accordion for her. Thinking the damaged accordion is good enough for a beginner, Sonia gives it to her little girl, Florry, who sticks chewing gum in the bellows as they are driving home from the contest.

A few years later Joey is mugged by three young Chinese Americans outside the Polish Club. Having inherited his father's and grandfather's prejudices along with their musical talents, he decides they should relocate to Texas to get away from "fuckin snow, chinks and niggers" (300), and they sell the green accordion at their MOVING TO TEXAS yard sale. A flash-forward reveals that Joey makes a "modest fortune" raising catfish and "ladybugs for the organic garden market" and remarries after Sonia's death in 1985.

"The Colors of Horses"

Josephine buys the accordion for three dollars at Joey and Sonia's yard sale, thinking it will be a good gift for Fay McGettigan, the old horse trainer who "had pretty much brought her up" (303) at her parents' ranch in Montana. She and her fiancé, Vergil Wheelwright, have been stopping at yard sales in every state they pass through and have picked up some incredible things, including "a painted plywood sign, BLESS THIS MESS . . . a faceless Infant of Prague . . . a twenty-pound cane encrusted with glassies and a leather pillow with the burned-in image of a running ostrich" (305). Proulx, who has written about the pleasure of shopping at yard sales and finding "useful books on all possible subjects,"[6] is commenting on the American consumer mentality: people buy things solely for the pleasure of spending money, and they cast away what they have bought without seeming to distinguish between valuable or useful things and junk—or for that matter between what can be fixed and what is damaged beyond repair.

Josephine and Vergil's journey from Chicago to Montana takes them through landscapes that bear evidence of this kind of throwaway mentality, beginning with a frightening trip through a Chicago ghetto like the "deep bad, unfixable" cities Ida has described earlier. They pass ice cream stands built on land held sacred by Native Americans. Unnaturally colored waste ponds sit next to a power plant that exudes different brightly colored vapors at various times of the day, ruining land that was once a beautiful prairie. Then Vergil points out "a baked white rock that should never have been touched, yet used as a military range, turned into a crusted landscape the texture of burned scrambled eggs but pierced with the deep holes of bomb craters, still strewn with wrecked trucks, some collapsed mowing machines and reapers, a bulldozer flaking into the pocked soil. Everything over there ruined, he said, to prove it could be ruined" (309). Along with their cultural heritage, the novel warns, Americans are losing their natural heritage through wanton disregard and active destruction.

The year is 1980. Josephine is returning home for the first time in five years, after a visit that ended badly and dealt the final blow to her already shaky marriage. Her husband, Simon Ults, killed her father's prize Appaloosa stallion, Umbrella Point. As Josephine explains the episode later to Vergil, Simon was not paying attention as her father, Kenneth, talked "on and on" about all the serious health problems that the horse might experience in the future, adding tearfully that, when the time came to euthanize Umbrella Point, he could not bear to kill the animal. Unfortunately, says Josephine, by the time Simon started listening, "Dad was making it seem like Umbrella already had all those things wrong with him and had to be put down and he couldn't do it" (330). Simon, she claims, shot the horse out of pity. In Kenneth's version of the story, however, Simon was "this silent, sulky bastard," who after shooting Umbrella Point, "comes up on the porch, still holding the rifle, and he starts to bring it up—oh there's no doubt in my mind he intended to shoot me, to shoot us all" (319). In response, Kenneth says, he shot Simon in one shoulder to defend himself and his family. Yet a comment by Josephine suggests a second, perhaps more powerful motive for her father's retaliation against Simon. By her estimate the horse would have lived another five or ten years, and, according to her father, it would have brought in more than fifty thousand dollars in stud fees during that time. Josephine blames Simon's guilt about the shooting for his subsequent affair and the break-up of their marriage. For years, she tells Vergil, she held her father responsible for the divorce.

Another dead horse also haunts Josephine's homecoming. The first sentence of "The Colors of Horses" explains: "Well, the horse had been buried, and then it had come back up, heaved out the earth by some sort of antigravity" (303). The horse is Old Egypt, the good-natured, much-loved gelding that Josephine rode as a child. Fay tells Josephine that Old Egypt was struck by lightning just two weeks before she arrived home, adding, "What I don't understand why he come back now. We dug one hell of a hole with the backhoe and it don't make sense. I think he wanted to see you one more time" (310). When she sees the horse, however, Josephine wishes Fay had not shown it to her—a feeling that reveals much about her general desire not to know unpleasant truths about herself and others. As the story progresses, Old Egypt comes to represent a whole series of buried truths, some of which pop up unexpectedly like the dead horse.

Josephine's father has based his whole life in Montana on a lie. Josephine's parents, Kenneth and Bette Switch, arrived in Montana from Boston in 1953 and bought a run-down ranch with money that Bette thought Kenneth had inherited but that he had actually embezzled from his employers, making him—like Octave earlier in the novel—another wealthy man who built his fortune on a criminal act.

Kenneth likes to tell people that when he and Bette started cattle ranching, they were "too ignorant to breathe without getting a lungful of dirt" (312). After a few years their herd developed brucellosis and had to be destroyed, driving them out of ranching for a few years, Kenneth took a job with a local horse auctioneer. He discovered that Appaloosa horses were beginning to increase in value because of efforts by several horse breeders to restore the breed "to its old glory as the great hunting and war horse of the plains" (313). He got into Appaloosa breeding while prices were still relatively low. On this second venture, he admits, "I was smart enough to know I didn't know anything," so he hired Fay McGettigan, who "knew horses—knows horses—like not many men do" (316). Fay, in fact, picked out Umbrella Point as the foundation for Kenneth's breeding program, and, as Kenneth says, that single two-hundred-dollar horse "made our living, he built this ranch" (318).

By 1980 Kenneth and Bette are wealthy enough to spend every winter in the Caribbean or the South Seas, while Fay tends the ranch and lives the life of an impoverished ranch hand. Though Josephine apparently never learns how her father got his start in the West, she does discover another unpleasant truth about Kenneth: a young woman who was in school with Josephine has recently given birth to his baby and is now charged with child abuse for knocking the infant off the bar at the VFW, where she was drinking. Josephine seems unconcerned about the gravely injured baby but extremely worried about the scandal: "[M]y father's name and part in all this was plastered across the evening news and every paper in the state. Me—I was the only one who didn't know" (329). Josephine's mother, Bette—one of these superficial people who ask questions but never listen to the answers—hopes the baby will die and tells Josephine that she plans to divorce Kenneth.

Josephine has relationship problems of her own. She knows that Vergil is divorced after "a bad marriage of crazy drinking, drugs, fighting and punch-ups," but she does not seem to give much thought to what these past actions might foretell for her marriage to him. Josephine dismisses them with, "He seemed to be over it" (303).

In fact, Vergil proves quickly that he is not over his excessive drinking. The day after they arrive at the ranch, Vergil and Fay get extremely drunk during a trip to town that quickly turns comic. Vergil does not even seem to be sexually attractive to Josephine, nor does he try to arouse her. Instead he tends to bully her into fulfilling his sexual desires by saying she must be frigid for not wanting to have sex with him. The day after Vergil and Fay's trip to town, the tensions in Josephine and Vergil's relationship finally become overt. Vergil says that Kenneth did the "right thing" in shooting Simon because her father believed "Simon was coming to blow everybody away." As for Simon's subsequent affair, he adds, "It happens all the time. And it's their fucking problem, not yours" (330).

Josephine tells Vergil that he is wrong, that he has no "moral balance" (330), but then she tries to smooth things over, suggesting a picnic. Yet something has changed between them: "Their affections had curdled. They were moving rapidly toward antipathies." On the picnic Vergil slaps her and roughly forces her to have sex, as—unknown to them—they are watched through binoculars by a masturbating Basque shepherd. Josephine is first aroused, but later enraged, by Vergil's actions, telling him, "That was rape" and refusing to agree when he replies that she "loved it." Vergil leaves the next morning, seeming "a little confused and hurt about the way things turned out" (331). In a flash-forward, however, the narrator explains that "his pose of decent uprightness was a false impression for he went to prison a few years later after bilking the credulous residents of a blue-chip nursing home through his fraudulent investment company promising large returns on stocks in selected 'environmentally sound corporations'" (331–32).

Josephine tells her parents that she is staying with them on the ranch, perhaps for good, because they have decided to remain married. Kenneth's infant daughter has died, and he has "signed up for fidelity counseling" (332). A flash-forward explains that within months Josephine marries a rancher who, a few years later develops the paranoid conviction that "the federal government was red-eyed out of control and a dark-skinned, bandy-legged United Nations takeover imminent, that a lack of school prayer had destroyed the American people's moral sense" (332). He and Josephine seal off their ranch and dig ten acres of bunkers and tunnels, creating their own underground city. Rooted in and at least in part motivated by racial and ethnic hatred, this subterranean existence is an extreme form of the avoidance Josephine seems to have practiced all her life. Their behavior may also be interpreted as a metaphor for the lifestyle of Josephine's parents and other wealthy people. When their social or physical environments become threatening, or even just unpleasant, they can afford to go elsewhere, or otherwise insulate themselves, leaving others behind to face circumstances they cannot avoid.

The history of Fay's family provides a sharp contrast to the lives of the self-indulgent escapists for whom Fay works. Proulx takes the reader back to the time of Fay's grandfather, Riley McGettigan, who left his impoverished family in Ireland in 1863, at age sixteen. Stealing the money to pay his steerage fare, he sailed for New York City, where he joined an Irish gang in time to take part in the July 1863 draft riot. That event, still considered one of the worst riots in American history, began as a protest by Irish laborers and street gangs over the "commutation clause" in the recently passed conscription law, which allowed men to avoid being drafted into the Union Army by paying $300, a price few Irish immigrants could afford. Many of them were also enraged by President Abraham Lincoln's Emancipation Proclamation, issued on 1 January 1863, because they feared that freed blacks would get the unskilled labor jobs that had been going to Irish immigrants. By the end of the week-long riot, hundreds of people, including many free African Americans, had been killed, and the mob had inflicted more than a million dollars in property damage, destroying the Colored Orphan Asylum and several brothels frequented by black sailors.[7] A hierarchy of racial hatred is again apparent. The Irish looked down on, and felt threatened by, freed blacks rising up from below. At the same time wealthy "Americans" put up signs reading "No Irish Need Apply" in their shops and factories and considered the Irish good only for tending to the dirty work of fighting the Civil War.

Later that summer, Riley, like many poor Irish immigrants, accepted money to be a wealthy man's substitute in the army. After the war, in which he served under General William Tecumseh Sherman during the march through Georgia, Riley re-enlisted and was sent to Fort Phil Kearny in Wyoming, leaving behind a new wife, who had decided not to accompany him because she was pregnant and afraid of Indians. In December 1866 an arrow wound in his neck convinced nineteen-year-old Riley that army life did not suit him after all. He deserted and went to Texas, where in 1879 he suffered a slow and grisly death, having been caught stealing cattle from "a rancher with a sense of humor" (337).

After shooting out Riley's elbows and knees to keep him from escaping, the ranch hands sewed him inside the hide of a freshly skinned cow and left him in the sun, saying they would be back in a month: "The hide shrank and dried in the heat of the day, tighter and tighter, while the nearby deliquescing carcass stank and attracted coyotes, their slavering and gnawing their night music, while in the beating day buzzards peppered the sky" (337). Yet another of the bizarre deaths scattered throughout *Accordion Crimes,* Riley's end is particularly horrifying because the murder is so carefully contrived.

Furthermore, as in the murders of the Italians in New Orleans and Kenneth's shooting of Simon, the underlying motivation for the rancher's vigilante "justice" is money: the price of a cow that in the eyes of its owner is worth more than the life of an Irishman.

Riley's wife, Mary, ended up married to an Irish railroad laborer in Montana. Her eldest child, Riley McGettigan Jr., worked as a ranch hand, remaining unmarried and saving his money until age forty, when he bought "a dry, scabby ranch" (337–38) and a seventeen-year-old mail-order bride from Ireland. Quick-tempered and a heavy drinker, Riley lost the ranch and deserted his wife, Maggie, and seven children when their son Fay, the eldest, was eleven years old. Maggie supported the family by taking in laundry. In San Francisco Riley "was struck down by a touring Cadillac with an electric self-starter" (338), one more in the string of bizarre deaths. Again, though it has an air of ironic poetic justice, the punishment seems too severe for the crime.

Maggie's legacy to her children is "a taste for song." Possessing true pitch, she accompanied her singing by playing a small accordion, "a tiny fingering diatonic she called a come-to-me-go-from-me": "Whatever befell her or them the woman had a song coiled in her lung for it, knew hundreds of verses and hundreds of tunes, remembered every sung fragment she ever heard, and had a quick knack for imitating birdcall" (338). Once a year, Fay takes his concertina to the home of his childless brother Padraic, his only surviving sibling. There the "two ugly, drunken, aging brothers with no gifts or grace beyond whiskey and music" (340) play and sing all they can remember of the songs they learned from their mother—keeping alive for just a little longer a musical heritage that will die with them.

Fay calls his father "a hard-luck feller," adding that he had "the natural luck of a McGettigan" (337). Fay seems to have inherited his father's luck. Early in life he concluded that he was "a poor, grace-less, homely and uneducated mick" (339), and he never married, living the lonely life of an impoverished ranch hand. A man with a gift for music and storytelling and a virtually untapped capacity for love, he is constrained by his own self-loathing as well as by poverty and ethnic prejudice.

Fay is disappointed in the green accordion, recognizing that it needs more repairs than he is able to handle. He eventually passes it on to Javier, an old Basque shepherd, who lives in a traditional round-topped Basque wagon while staying with the sheep in mountain pastures during the summer. In Montana the Basques seem to be at the bottom of the social ladder. Fay and the other ranch hands tell Basque jokes instead of polack jokes in the local bar.

A people of the western Pyrenees with a language and culture distinct from that of the rest of Spain, the Basques have been shepherds for centuries. Yet Fay mentions that Javier is the only one of his people who follows the old way of life; sheep ranchers are hiring Mexicans and Peruvians instead, and the old sheep wagons are becoming yard decorations or ending up in museums. Fay arrives to visit Javier during a festival at which the musicians play old Basque music on traditional instruments, including the accordionlike *trikitixa*. The musicians, however, are probably from Los Angeles, not local Basques. Their old culture is in the process of fading away.

Javier begins repairing the accordion, but before he gets to replace the bellows, and thus find the hidden money, he too suffers a bizarre death. Picking up the green accordion from the ground where he set it a few hours earlier, he disturbs a rattlesnake that has crawled under the bellows to sleep and suffers a fatal snake bite. His possessions are stored at the Basque hotel where he used to spend his winters, and two years later anything that seems salable, including the green accordion, is sent to the Little Boy Blue Pawnshop to be sold on commission.

"Back Home with Reattached Arms"

The last, and shortest, section of *Accordion Crimes* is set in Old Glory, Minnesota, an ironically named town that serves as a nightmarish epitome of the nation as a whole. Hidden riches and danger lie buried beneath the surface while the townspeople live a zombielike existence caught in a meaningless cycle of consumerism.

Nils Gasmann likes to tell the story of how his father and uncles hit a vein of copper while digging a well on the family farm. Intent on finding water, they took some samples that they planned to send to an assayer, and kept digging. The package was never sent and was eventually lost. Nils curses the "stubbornness and single-track minds" of "those old Norwegian fools" (349), but he never digs near the old well to see what he might find.

There is something ominous underground as well. People have claimed for years that they hear "a low-pitched hum coming from underground," a fact confirmed by scientists in the 1970s. Unable to ascertain the cause, they label it "scientifically intriguing" (362). They also discover dangerous levels of radon gas, an element generated by the radioactive decay of radium, which in turn is created by the decay of uranium. The leakage of radon into the residents' basements explains the extraordinarily high cancer rate in Old Glory. The mysterious humming seems to be the cause of another local problem: "The town's fatigue rate was far above the national average; men slumped for long periods of time in front of their television sets, women lurched to their jobs, nodding off in commuter vans" (362). When they learn about the radon hazard, many of the townspeople move away, leaving a virtual wasteland.

Seen in the context of the entire novel, Old Glory becomes a powerful and frightening metaphor for the United States: the cultural heritages of its people lie buried and forgotten, while smoldering just below the surface, ready to erupt in violence, is a reservoir of anger and hatred generated by a longstanding tradition of racial and ethnic prejudice. Old Glory seems to be sitting atop a natural atomic bomb, poised for figurative, if not literal, explosion. Meanwhile, people go about their lives hypnotized by media messages promoting consumerism and conveying a false picture of American life that ignores "unpleasant" truths, whether racism or environmental hazards.

They are out of touch with their natural surroundings, the sky as well as the land. At one point Ivar Gasmann echoes Ben Rainwater in *Postcards,* musing: "Here we got a whole country afraid of the dark, millions of people never seen the stars or sky except on TV." This fear has created a "sucking need for light," and the result is the construction of more and more power plants that burn up natural resources: "Trees, fluids, gases, ores, air, sunlight, all transmuted to blades of light whetted to lance the black boil of night" (358).

The Gasmann family of Old Glory is Proulx's final, and most grotesque, example of melting-pot acculturation. Gunnar Gasmann, who arrived from Norway in 1902, bought farmland in Old Glory in 1912—land that had already been clear cut by loggers. Gunnar and his wife tried to pass on Norwegian language and traditions to their children, but their son, Nils, forbids his sons to learn Norwegian, because "Norwegians were a joke and their accent was a joke and they made themselves into jokes with low comedy acts and songs" (348). Thus, displaying the typical first-generation American's desire to fit into mainstream "American" society, Nils throws away everything that is good about his ancestors' culture because some aspects of it embarrass him.

By the time his son Conrad is an adult there are new ethnic groups to hate, "chinks and spics, and pakis and those aye-rabs." Conrad complains to a neighbor, "It's not the same thing as when our grandparents come over; they were white, they had guts, a good work ethic. . . . [T]he country's filled up, there's not enough room, not enough jobs to go around" (365–66). Again, Proulx demonstrates a fact of life that has existed at least since the mid–nineteenth century: as each successive group of immigrants pushes up from the bottom of the ladders, those on the rungs just above become afraid of losing their places in society and react with prejudice toward the newcomers.

The victim of a lumbering accident in which a small boulder hit him in the head, Nils Gasmann has a "savage, volatile personality" (348). In a comic scene that lightens the foreboding tone of the narrative, Nils, who has been drinking heavily, becomes so enraged at a woodpecker rapping on his roof while he is trying to sleep that his efforts to get rid of the bird end up setting fire to the roof and destroying the entire second story of the house. Funny as it is, the episode is also a parable about the corrosive power of anger on reason and compassion. Nils rebuilds the second story, but after discovering that he has cut the stringer for the stairs too short, he angrily refuses to buy more lumber. He forces the family to use a ladder to get to the second floor, suggesting a permanent difficulty of access to higher faculties such as rationality and caring.

The targets of Nils's anger are most often his sons, Conrad and Ivar. In fact, he nearly kills Ivar in what begins as another humorous episode, which also includes some pointed social commentary. In 1951, when Ivar is seven, Nils allows Howard Poplin, an itinerant preacher, and his family to set up their folding plywood house and church on Gasmann land. As Howard explains, the house is "designed to travel, to be set down in this system of traveling house parks right across the country, a national system, all alike"; though these parks have not been established yet, he adds, "they will be after Eisenhower's road system gits finished" (350). The interstate highway system begun by the federal government in the 1950s is widely recognized as one of the factors that increased Americans' mobility after the Second World War, and, with the rise of manufactured housing and mobile-home parks during the second half of the century, Howard's prediction that in ten years half the United States will be living in plywood "travel houses" like his is a humorous exaggeration that includes some truth.

Playing on the 1950s enthusiasm for all things atomic, which was fueled by a national media campaign promoting the peacetime uses of atomic power and downplaying the potential danger of radiation leakage, Howard's church is called the Atomic Power Church—a name with ominous overtones suggesting the long-term consequence of Howard's religion. Creeping down to the church to investigate Howard's late-night services, Nils discovers to his horror that Howard is a snake-handling faith healer and is even more shocked when Howard "heals" Ivar of the polio he has never had. Ivar is paid five dollars for his slick acting job, setting in motion his life-long monomania for acquiring money.

Nils is so enraged that he drags Ivar back to the barn and beats him nearly to death with a rusty chain. Finally Nils's wife, Elise, hits her husband over the head with a crowbar to stop the beating. She believes she has killed Nils, but Howard, who has arrived with a snake wrapped around his neck, prays and wraps the snake around Nils for the rest of the night. The next morning the two men emerge from the barn, Nils wrapped in the snake and announcing his conversion to the Atomic Power Church. Over the years he continues to handle snakes and even puts pinches of rat killer in his tea, convinced that his faith protects him.

A flash-forward reveals that Howard has become rich by investing money donated to the church in a camper he named *The Conqueror* and has retired to Florida, where he "calls himself Happy Jack" (355). Perhaps the most cynical of the self-inventors in the novel, Howard/Happy Jack has made a fortune by preying on the gullible and emotionally vulnerable, encouraging self-delusion and recklessness.

While Nils's conversion gives him a sense of invincibility, it does not extend to forgiveness. Elise sends "wordless and cringing" Ivar and "impatient and clumsy" Conrad to live with her sister, but she stays with Nils, who waits for the right time to inflict his idea of justice on his "murderer" (355). Twenty years later as Elise lies in bed dying of cancer, Nils's anger at her moaning overcomes his "guilt and pity." He murders her with an axe, climbs the silo—where years earlier he painted a huge "picture of Jesus with a snake in each hand standing in front of a house trailer"—and jumps with the humorously ambiguous thought "that Jesus would be there to catch him or there would be hell to pay" (404). Having become the grotesque embodiment of his irrational anger, Nils disproves his invincibility with his final act.

The farm is left to both sons, but Ivar sells his share to Conrad, who in turn sells all but four acres and the house and keeps his job at the gas company. He jokes to his daughter that he has to work there because his name is Gasmann. To the people of Old Glory, Ivar seems mentally retarded, "slow in mind and dirty in person" and "soft, yet potentially violent" (345). He pushes a shopping cart around town like a derelict, picking up unwanted things that women set out for him. Yet Ivar has an uncanny knack for making money by selling the townspeople's "trash" to tourists and travelers. Then in 1988 he buys the contents of a musty old funeral home for one dollar from the owner's only heir, who considers the house and everything in it worthless. By knowing where to look for hidden cash and where to find markets for the furnishings, Ivar clears $111,999 on his investment and uses the money to start a fantastically successful used-furniture and antiques business. By 1992 he owns a Montana ranch and a Tahiti beach house, but he still looks and acts like a homeless person and continues to wander around Old Glory picking up trash.

On one of his buying trips Ivar purchases the contents of the Little Boy Blue Pawnshop, including the green accordion. In this case, however, his uncanny ability to find hidden money fails him. He consigns the accordion to the one-dollar table at his Old Glory warehouse store.

A man who has "never had sexual intercourse with a woman" and has only "ambivalent" feelings about men (345), Ivar has no

interests apart from making money and no sense of social responsibility; indeed, he exists entirely apart from society. Amoral rather
than immoral, he is an idiot savant of capitalism, a grotesque caricature of the 1980s investors who made huge fortunes but did not
reinvest their profits in the American economy. The great irony of
Ivar's wealth, of course, is that, like Octave, Ivar has based his
financial empire on other people's refuse.

Conrad Gasmann is not as lucky as his brother. One windy day
while his young daughter, Vela, is waving a broom at swallows in
the yard, a piece of jagged, inadequately anchored scrap metal blows
off a passing truck and cuts off both her arms. Though doctors reat-
tach her arms they are essentially useless. By the time she returns
home, she has developed a love for accordion music, including the
"champagne music" of Lawrence Welk, which her father describes
to his friend Dick Cude as "stale before I was born" (366).

Dick sees the dusty green accordion in Ivar's store and buys it
for Vela, thinking that although she cannot play it, she will enjoy
looking at it. When he gets it home, he ruins it by washing it in the
kitchen sink but decides to give it to her anyway. He also sends
along a big bag of accordion tapes. Unfortunately, Vela receives
Dick's gifts while girls from school are visiting her. Because they
like only hip-hop and make fun of accordion music, she tells her
mother to throw away all the tapes and the green accordion. The
pathetically grotesque Vela represents the last vestige of hope for a
long tradition of music in danger of being lost forever. The irony of
the situation is apparent: robbed of her heritage as surely as she has
been robbed of the use of her arms, she—and by extension her entire
generation—have had the power to carry on traditions taken from
them by parents who have no interest in passing them on.

By an ironic twist of fate, the next owner of the accordion is Whitey Kunky, who was with his father in the truck carrying the scrap metal that cut off Vela's arms. Now a garbageman, Whitey finds the green accordion and takes it with him in the cab of the truck carrying Old Glory's garbage to a landfill in Mississippi. As he tells the story of Vela's accident to his companion in the truck, Whitey begins to cry, becomes angry at his "childish weakness and to get back to normal again" he throws the accordion from the truck "into a wasteland of shacks and weeds" (377). Once again, and for the last time, anger determines the fate of the accordion.

Three little black boys of about four or five find one of the thousand dollar bills from the accordion beside the road and use it to pay for sodas in a rundown grocery store, where the shocked and honest proprietor tells them to tell their mother that "she got change comin" (381). On the way home the boys find the accordion. Never realizing that it is the source of the money, they throw it in front of an eighteen-wheeler, which runs over the instrument, "and in its gritty wash fluttered thousand-dollar bills" (381). The boys run away, unaware of the fortune they are leaving behind.

Accordion Crimes offers a grim prognosis for the state of the American Dream. One of the epigraphs to the novel is a quotation from Cornel West's *Race Matters* (1993): "Without the presence of black people in America, European-Americans would not be 'white'—they would be only Irish, Italians, Poles, Welsh, and others engaged in class, ethnic, and gender struggles over resources and identity." As successive European immigrant groups have climbed the social-economic ladder through acculturation they have left behind a vast, mostly black underclass on which to focus an enduring racial prejudice. Racial inequality is alive and well while ethnic and regional cultural differences are being erased by a vast mediocre pop culture spread by the mass media. If the novel holds out any hope at all, it may be for African American music, which has had a formative influence on mainstream American music throughout the twentieth century. It is ironic that, because their community is excluded from mainstream society, some of their traditions are not lost.

Another disturbing theme in the novel is the randomness of characters' fates, which is especially apparent in the many bizarre deaths in the novel. From the accordion maker through Javier the Basque shepherd, few characters die natural deaths. Some, such as Beutle and Dolor, die as a result of their obsessions. Others, including Beutle's grandson, Warfield Dunks, and Hieronim/Harry, die as a result of clumsiness or stupidity. Yet others—the accordion maker and his son, Riley McGettigan and Riley Jr., and Javier—are the victims of random occurrences or historical forces that are neither of their making nor within their control. *Accordion Crimes* asserts that there is neither justice nor design in the universe beyond what meager controls human beings choose to exert on their lives.

CHAPTER SIX

Close Range: Wyoming Stories

Illustrated with six watercolors by William Matthews that complement her themes, Proulx's 1999 collection of short stories depicts people trying to survive on the "[d]angerous and indifferent ground"[1] of the American West. In a book where descriptions of the beautiful but forbidding landscape frequently create a lyrical counterpoint to the violence and tragedy of individual lives, perhaps the most eloquent description of Wyoming comes at the beginning of the starkly tragic "People in Hell Just Want a Drink of Water": "You stand there, braced. Cloud shadows race over the buff rock stacks as a projected film, casting a queasy mottled ground rash. The air hisses and it is no local breeze but the great harsh sweep of wind from the turning of the earth. The wild country—indigo jags of mountains, grassy plains everlasting, tumbled stones like fallen cities, the flaring roll of sky—provokes a spiritual shudder. It is like a deep note that cannot be heard but is felt, it is like a claw in the gut" (97). Against this backdrop individual human beings and even whole civilizations are negligible indeed, and the only human approach to such overwhelming forces is a healthy dose of fiction. As Proulx explains in her acknowledgments, the epigraph to the book—"Reality's never been much use out here"—is a quotation from an anonymous retired Wyoming rancher. Instances of magical realism occur throughout the stories. As Proulx writes, "The elements of unreality, the fantastic and improbable, color all of these stories as they color real life. In Wyoming not the least fantastic situation is the determination to make a living ranching in this tough and unforgiving place" (9).

"The Half-Skinned Steer"

In her acknowledgments Proulx writes that the idea for writing a collection of stories set in Wyoming came from an invitation by the Nature Conservancy to contribute a story inspired by a visit to one of its preserves to an anthology of short fiction titled *Off the Beaten Path* (1998). The result of Proulx's visit to the Ten Sleep Preserve on the south slope of the Big Horn Mountains in Wyoming was "The Half-Skinned Steer," first published in the November 1997 issue of the *Atlantic Monthly* and later selected by Garrison Keillor for inclusion in *The Best American Short Stories of 1998* and by John Updike for the best-selling *The Best American Short Stories of the Century* (1999). In his introduction to that anthology Updike describes Proulx's story as revisiting "the West that has seemed to this country the essence of itself." He adds, "I would have liked to finish this volume with a choice less dark, with an image less cruel and baleful than that of a half-skinned steer, but the American experience, story after story insisted, has been brutal and hard."[2]

"The Half-Skinned Steer" follows the journey of Mero, a well-to-do man in his eighties, who makes an ill-advised cross-country journey from his home in Massachusetts to Wyoming for the funeral of his brother, Rollo, whom he has not seen in sixty years. He sets out to return to the family ranch he left in 1936. It is now a successful tourist attraction: Down Under Wyoming, where Rollo has been killed by the sharp claws of an emu, a nonindigenous bird brought there by the Australian co-owners of the park.

Mero's trek evokes the traditional, mythic associations of the westward journey toward death, as he makes his solitary pilgrimage back in time as well as distance toward his boyhood home. Overestimating his diminished capacities as a driver, he causes an accident near Des Moines, totaling his Cadillac. He buys another and drives resolutely onward, only to become lost and stuck during a snowstorm just miles from his destination, where he discovers that all his efforts to stave off death through a healthy vegetarian diet and vigorous exercise are of no avail against the powerful forces of nature.

As he travels, Mero remembers the situation that precipitated his leaving home at twenty-three: the sexual longing aroused in him by his father's girlfriend and her telling of a grisly tall tale about a botched slaughter of a steer. In her story—which, according to Proulx is based on an Icelandic folktale called "Porgeir's Bull"—a hard-luck rancher, called Tin Head because of the metal plate in his head, sets out to butcher a steer, hitting it on the head with an axe and stunning instead of killing it. Thinking the animal dead, he hangs it up to bleed out for a while and then begins to skin it, starting with the head. Halfway through the job, he stops for dinner, after cutting out the steer's tongue so his wife can cook his favorite dish.

When he returns to finish the job, the half-skinned steer is gone. As he scans the horizon, "in the west on the side of the mountain he sees something moving stiff and slow" with "something bunchy and wet hanging down over its hindquarters." As the mute steer turns and looks back at him, Tin Head sees "the empty mouth without no tongue open wide and its red eyes glaring at him, pure teetotal hatred like arrows coming at him, and he knows he is done for and all of his kids is done for, and that his wife is done for" (35)—and, the girlfriend explains, his intuition proves true.

This powerful story, with its pathetic and grotesque image of the death that comes for every living being, has turned Mero into a vegetarian, but it has also had another, greater impact on his life, as it has become associated with the sexual longings evoked in him by its teller. After hearing her tale, Mero "dreamed of horse breeding or hoarse breathing, whether the act of sex or bloody cut-throat gasps he didn't know" (23). Years later he is still troubled by his dream, from which he awoke with the conviction that it was time to leave home. For a long time he believed that he had no "hard reason" for going off on his own, but at eighty-three he favors the straightforward explanation "that it had been time for him to find his own territory and his own woman," and he congratulates himself on having "married three or four of them and sampled plenty" (31). Yet the alluring sexuality of his father's girlfriend and her gruesome story have become permanently linked in his mind, creating a simultaneous attraction and aversion to the opposite sex. As he travels into the country of his boyhood, he is still haunted by memories of the woman who "could make you smell the smoke from an unlit fire" (33) and the image of the half-skinned steer, which clearly symbolizes the death he has worked so hard to avoid.

As he reaches the vicinity of the ranch at nightfall, falling snow and the absence of long-remembered landmarks confuse Mero. He turns on a narrow track that may or may not lead to the ranch, and his car becomes stuck in the snow. Ignoring his first impulse to wait in the car until morning, he exerts himself in an unsuccessful attempt to free the car. Then he begins walking through the snowstorm in the direction where he thinks he will find a neighboring ranch about ten miles away—if the house is still there and if he is correct in his intuition of his present location.

As he walks through "the violent country," feeling vulnerable in the wind and cold, he notices that one animal in a herd of cattle on the other side of a fence is walking with him. As he turns to look at it, he realizes that "he'd been wrong again, that the half-skinned steer's red eye had been watching him all this time" (37–38). Coming face to face with his own mortality, Mero learns that neither money nor healthy living can insulate him from the traumas of his past or the inevitability of death. As he takes his final walk, "feeling as easy to tear as a man cut from paper" (37), he has become like the half-skinned steer, robbed of all defenses against the forces of nature and stumbling mute and vulnerable toward death.

Though "The Half-Skinned Steer" is a story about an ending, it is also about returning to one's beginning, where, stripped bare of all defenses, one faces the harsh realities of life. As such, the story is a fitting introduction to a collection of short stories in which character after character faces an unforgiving environment, feeling as vulnerable as "a man cut from paper."

"The Mud Below"

First published in the 22 June 1998 issue of the *New Yorker,* "The Mud Below" follows the career of a young rodeo bullrider, Diamond Felts, of Red Sled, Wyoming, who, at five foot three, has been called derogatory nicknames such as "Half-Pint" and "Shorty" all his life. Constantly at odds with his mother, Kaylee, Diamond has been rejected by the only man he has known as father. Shirley Felts left Kaylee when Diamond was thirteen, telling the boy, "Not your father and never was" (65). As a result of this emotional trauma, Diamond is as stunted emotionally as he is physically—his outward appearance mirroring the inner self.

Unlike most of the rodeo performers he meets, Diamond was not brought up on a ranch or in a rodeo family. He discovered bullriding in the spring of his senior year in high school, when his classmate Leecil Bewd suggested Diamond and a friend could make some extra money by helping out at the Bewd family ranch during calf branding. When the work was done, Diamond rode a bull for the first time: "The shock of the violent motion, the lightning shifts of balance, the feeling of power as though he were a bull and not the rider, even the fright, fulfilled some greedy physical hunger in him he hadn't known was there. The experience had been exhilarating and unbearably personal" (47). His identification with the bull introduces an important theme in the story as Diamond, for the first time in his life, experienced a sense of power over others.

Going against his mother's wish that he attend college, he enrolls at a bullriding school and then sets out on the rodeo circuit with Leecil, who quits after their first season to go home to help his ailing father on the ranch, which he and his brothers ultimately lose because of exorbitant inheritance taxes. Neither a knee injury nor his mother's taking him to visit a brain-damaged one-time-champion bronc rider, however, can persuade Diamond to quit bullriding.

Shirley Felts's parting disclaimer has created a secret resentment in Diamond against his mother and made him wary of other human relationships as well. He sees women as useful only for sex, going through a long series of one-night stands and even raping the wife of his second traveling partner, Martin Sasser. For Diamond sex is "a half-hour painkiller" but bullriding "gave him the indescribable rush, shot him mainline with crazy-ass elation" (65). Unable to cope with the rejection and emotional turmoil he has experienced outside the rodeo arena, Diamond has transferred all his love to bullriding and made rodeo his whole world.

His next traveling partner, Pake Bitts, "a big Jesus-loving steer roper" (66) who turns out to be Myron Sasser's half brother, takes

Diamond to task for his treatment of women, explaining "the bull is not supposed to be your role model, he is your opponent and you have to get the better of him" (68). The remark establishes a metaphorical connection between the bull and unbridled libido. Yet Diamond insists the bull is "my partner" (68), demonstrating his unwillingness, and even inability, to see Pake's point. As Pake says, Diamond "don't get how it is for nobody but your own dee self. You don't get it that you can't have a fence with only one post" (69). Diamond is so focused on himself and his pain that he cannot establish, or even understand, close human relationships.

Later in the season, he gets drunk in a bar where other rodeo men are talking about their families and offers his own views on the subject: "You all make a big noise about family . . . , but none of you spend much time at home and you never wanted to or you wouldn't be in rodeo. Rodeo's family. Ones back at the ranch don't count for shit" (71). However, after he suffers a painful shoulder dislocation in a bullriding accident, Diamond feels the need to confront the issue at the heart of his rejection of family. A phone call to his mother elicits the exclamation that Shirley Felts has "set you [Diamond] up like a time bomb" (77), but no clear indication of whether Shirley is Diamond's father.

Diamond's painful injury has destroyed his passion for bullriding, Later, remembering a ranch hand castrating calves at the Bewd ranch, he thinks, "The course of life's events seemed slower than the knife but not less thorough" (78). He also recalls his mother's having once said that she had given up "everything" for him and finally seems to have an inkling of what she meant: that the arguments that precipitated the break-up of her marriage were over Diamond. "It was all a hard fast ride that ended in the mud," Diamond decides, but as he drives through the night, he begins to rekindle at least a small part of his passion for bullriding: "Very slowly, as slowly as light comes on a clouded morning, the euphoric heat flushed through him, or maybe just the memory of it" (78). In realizing that personal gratification has a price, he has finally, perhaps, taken a first step on the long road to adulthood.

"Job History"

A brief, minimalist story told by a laconic third-person narrator, "Job History" chronicles the struggles of Leeland and Lori Lee to support their growing family, mostly in the ironically named town of Unique, Wyoming. The Lees' story is set against the backdrop of historical events from the civil rights movement of the 1960s and the Vietnam War through the Super Bowl game of 1990. After dropping out of high school at seventeen, in 1964, to marry the pregnant Lori, Leland goes through a series of dead-end jobs and unsuccessful business ventures. Many of them fail as a result of historical or environmental forces beyond his control. The gas station where he finds his first job goes out of business after a new interstate highway bypasses Unique, which was on the major route to Yellowstone National Park. Later he and his father go bankrupt when an unusually cold winter destroys their hog business; and during the recession of the 1980s he and Lori have to give up their meat-locker operation, because the owners of small ranches go back to butchering and cutting their own beef to save money.

Other failures are the result of poor business decisions. For example, Leland and Lori start a ranch supply business in the old gas station, thinking that local people will be happy to shop there rather than make a long trip into town; they discover, however, that people "relish the drive to a bigger town" (83). Later their gas station/convenience store in the same building again fails because of location.

By the end of the story Lori has died and Leland is working as a short-order cook. He and his eldest son are dreaming of starting an ill-conceived combination motorcycle repair shop and steak house in the same old gas station where Leland has had two earlier failures, and "[n]obody has time to listen to the news" (87). As the reader of *Accordion Crimes* will recognize, Leland and Lori's experiences are far from unique. Lacking the financial resources that might buffer them during economic downturns, they and their family and neighbors, like so many other Americans, live at the mercy of historical forces they do not understand.

"The Blood Bay"

First published in the 28 December 1998–4 January 1999 issue of the *New Yorker,* "The Blood Bay" is as fantastic and grotesquely comic as "Job History" is realistic and matter-of-fact. The brief story is Proulx's Wyoming version of an old folktale, "The Calf That Ate the Traveler."

During the cold winter of 1886–87 three cowboys happen on another who has frozen to death. The comically named Dirt Sheets takes a fancy to the dead man's handmade boots and, discovering that they are frozen to the corpse's feet, he saws them off with the feet and lower legs still in them. Later the cowboys spend the night in a shack with an old man, Grice, and his two horses. Sheets, who has left his "grisly trophies" behind the stove, rises before the others, removes the boots from the thawed feet, and heads for town to "telegraph a filial sentiment to his mother on her birthday" (93).

Grice finds the severed limbs and Sheets's old boots in the corner where Sheets has put them and comes to the conclusion that his "spirited" blood-bay horse must have eaten Sheets. He is horrified but also "pleased to own a horse with the sand to eat a raw cowboy" (94). Sheets's friends, who know full well the origin of the feet, do nothing to dissuade the old man from his illusions, especially when he offers to pay them all his money, a little more than forty dollars to keep quiet about his "man-eating" horse. They do not even tell the story to Sheets when they see him that evening, nor do they offer to share the money with him, since, according to their self-interested assessment, "The arithmetic stood comfortable" (94). That is, Sheets gets new boots, and his friends profit financially.

As in most tall tales, the humor in "The Blood Bay" comes from exaggeration, including the sharp contrasts within characters' sensibilities. For example, Sheets thinks nothing of dismembering a corpse for a pair of boots and casually discarding the limbs, but he is so sentimental about his mother that he is willing to "ride faster than chain lightning with the links snapped" (93) in bitterly cold weather to reach a telegraph office in time to wire her birthday greetings. Grice is shocked at his blood bay's supposed "breakfast," but he cares more about the horse than its presumed human victim.

"People in Hell Just Want a Drink of Water"

First published in the April 1999 issue of *GQ,* the fifth story in *Close Range* contrasts two ranch families living on the "[d]angerous and indifferent ground" of Wyoming, where "tragedies of people count for nothing although signs of misadventure are everywhere" (97).

Isaac "Ice" Dunmire from Texas, who staked out a homestead and built a sod shanty in 1909, raises his nine sons alone after his wife leaves him in 1913, losing one to encephalitis and bringing up the others "to fill his labor needs" (99). Under his spartan regime they learn to work hard, endure pain, and consider themselves superior to those who are weaker than they.

By the Depression of the 1930s, a period of drought in the western plains, the brothers are well established: "The country, its horses and cattle suited them and if they loved anything that was it, and they ran that country because there were eight of them and Ice and they were of one mind." Uneducated about anything unrelated to ranching, they have "measured beauty and religion by what they rode through everyday, and this encouraged their disdain for art and intellect. There was a somber arrogance about them, a rigidity of attitude that said theirs was the only way" (101). They are so hardened by their upbringing that they are largely incapable of what they would call the "soft" emotions of love or compassion.

Horace Tinsley, from St. Louis, has come west hoping for easy success, but he has failed at three livestock ventures. An impractical dreamer, he admires the scenic aspects of his land but has little talent for putting the land to use. His neighbors like him for his "kindly manner" and musical skills, but look on "him with contemptuous pity for his loose control of home affairs and his coddling of a crazy wife after her impetuous crime" (102). On the long trip into Laramie, his unstable, sensitive wife became so deranged by the incessant crying of their infant daughter that she threw the child into the Little Laramie River, where the baby drowned.

The remorseful Mrs. Tinsley turns into a grotesque caricature of the neurotically overprotective mother. She is vigilant with her two remaining children, even "tying them to the chairs in the kitchen lest they wander outside and come to harm" (102). Under her suffocating restrictions, the Tinsleys' son, Rasmussen (called Ras), develops his intellectual interests. Fascinated with trains and ships and longing to travel, he leaves home at sixteen and does not write to his parents.

Five years later, in 1933, Ras is back home, having got as far as Schenectady, New York, where he was in a serious automobile accident that has left him horribly disfigured, brain damaged, and nearly mute. His only pleasure is riding his fourteen-year-old horse—and, his shocked parents soon discover, exposing his penis and making suggestive gestures to young women on neighboring ranches. He may look like a "monster" and act like a "half-wit," but he still has the sexual urges of a young man.

Displaying the typical Dunmire confidence in the rightness of his convictions, Jaxon, the eldest son, indirectly threatens Horace about Ras: "There's some around who'd as soon cut him and make sure he don't breed any more half-wits, calm him down some" (112). Tinsley starts to speak to Ras, but—indecisive as usual—he hesitates, not wanting to increase his son's unhappiness. When he finally warns Ras about the Dunmires, Ras laughs at him. The Dunmires have castrated the young man with a dirty knife, and by the time Horace discovers what they have done, Ras is dying of gangrene—leaving the reader to ponder the possibility that the emotionally stunted Dunmires are as inwardly grotesque as Ras is outwardly disfigured.

The story ends with the narrator's unsuccessful attempt to assert that times have changed:

> That was all sixty years ago and more. Those hard days
> are finished. . . . We are in a new millennium and such
> desperate things no longer happen.
>   If you believe that you'll believe anything. (115)

Standing alongside this harsh view of human nature is Proulx's lyrical evocation of place. At the beginning of the story the narrator marvels that through all the cruelties human beings have inflicted on each other, nothing "delays the flood of morning light." In contrast nothing man-made will last for long: "Other cultures have camped here a while and disappeared. Only earth and sky matter. Only the endlessly repeated flood of morning light. You begin to see that God does not owe us much beyond that" (97). As Ras lies dying, the narration echoes this early passage: "The morning light flooded the rim of the world, poured through the window glass, colored the wall and floor, laid its yellow blanket on the reeking bed, the kitchen table and the cups of cold coffee" (115).

It is a hard, unforgiving light, baking the drought-ridden land as swarms of grasshoppers hit against the house. Yet it is also as beautiful as the "wild country" on which it shines. Proulx's reverence and respect for this "[d]angerous and indifferent ground" is suffused throughout the story and lightens its pessimism about the essential nature of humankind, which, against the long duration of geological time, counts for little.

"The Bunchgrass Edge of the World"

While the story that precedes it is an essentially tragic story occasionally lightened by bits of ironic humor, "The Bunchgrass Edge of the World," first published in the 30 November 1998 issue of the *New Yorker,* is a mostly comic look at human folly and self-delusion set against the same unforgiving Wyoming landscape. The main character, Ottaline Touhey, a young woman "distinguished by a physique approaching the size of a hundred-gallon propane tank" (123), resembles the comic grotesque failures one finds in Flannery O'Connor's fiction; but Ottaline, like Quoyle before her, succeeds in finding a measure of happiness against improbable odds.

Ottaline's father, the youngest son of old Red Touhey, is named Aladdin after the brand of lamp that arrived from Sears, Roebuck on the day in 1946 when he was born. After developing a love of flying as a pilot in the Vietnam War, he returns home to marry a girl with an equally comic name, Wauneta Hipsag. At their wedding the guests throw wheat instead of rice, and back at the Touhey ranch a few grains fall from Aladdin's pants cuff onto the ground near the porch, reseeding and spreading as the years pass. Wauneta calls this grain, which eventually covers a quarter of an acre, her "wedding wheat" and predicts that, if it were ever cut, "the world would end" (121). Her warning is metaphorically prophetic but on a smaller scale than she imagines; by the end of the story the wheat has been mown down, and her life with Aladdin has been cut short.

When Aladdin is twenty-six, he wrests control of the ranch from his father, whom Wauneta moves from the big upstairs bedroom to a small, former pantry off the kitchen. She feels no love for the old man, especially after she interprets his play with four-year-old Ottaline as an attempt to molest the child. Wauneta hopes old Red will die soon, but old Red continues to persevere, "determined to make his century" (123), as she and Aladdin age and their three children finish high school.

CLOSE RANGE: WYOMING STORIES

Only Ottaline stays on the ranch, where she surprises her father with her talent for working with animals and her ability to handle heavy ranch work. But her longing becomes intense, and the story veers into magical realism. In an old quarry where her father has dumped worn-out tractors, she begins to hear a "treacherous John Deere 4030" (129), which once killed a ranch hand, talking to her. The tractor keeps after her until it finally gets its way with her. Once she has climbed into its seat, "feeling an awful thrill" (137), she convinces Aladdin that they should haul the tractor into a shed and attempt the major repair work necessary to get it running again.

Ottaline's "love affair" with the tractor ends abruptly, however, when she has to substitute for her sick father during the annual visit of Amendinger the cattle buyer to offer them a price for their stock. Amendinger's "big-nostriled, heavyset" son, Flyby, comes instead (141). He is impressed by Ottaline's knowledge of cattle, gives her a good price, and invites her to have a beer with him. That night, having observed earlier that the wedding wheat should be cut, Flyby mows it down with a scythe while Ottaline watches from the door to the tractor shed, tossing tractor parts into the air.

By the time of Ottaline and Flyby's wedding the following September, the tractor has been dumped in a ditch outside the ranch fence. Though Aladdin and Wauneta do not realize it at first, a new generation is gradually starting to take over the ranch. The climactic moment comes after Aladdin buys a new airplane and expects the whole family to be there when he lands it in a pasture—even the reluctant Flyby, who does "not like living under the thumb of Aladdin Touhey" (145). Flyby's feeling echoes Aladdin's sentiments about old Red decades earlier. As Aladdin shows off for the family, Wauneta shouts "YOU GET DOWN HERE!" (145), and

Aladdin promptly crashes the plane, killing himself in the process. Ottaline irrationally blames her father's death on her mother's shouting, while Wauneta offers the equally improbable, but symbolically apt, explanation that cutting the wedding wheat was the cause. Old Red has the last word on the subject, however: "He done it hisself" (146).

The story ends with the old man's self-satisfied thoughts about the future. He is sure that once Aladdin is buried Wauneta will move to Las Vegas to be near her other two children, leaving Ottaline and "her scytheman" to run the ranch and old Red free to move back upstairs. Finally, he concludes: "The main thing in life was staying power. That was it: stand around long enough you'd get to sit down" (146). Now ninety-six years old, he may well "make his century," but the one certainty in the world of these stories is that the wild, "indifferent ground" of Wyoming will survive him, as generation after generation passes away.

"Pair a Spurs"

Set in the recent past, circa 1998, the long story "Pair a Spurs" depicts the fates of two ranches and their owners at a time so bleak that it seems possible that the end of the world is imminent. The theme is reinforced by a millenarian metalsmith who makes a "bad luck" pair of spurs. Yet the spurs also add an element of magical realism and contribute to the ironic comedy that runs throughout the story.

"Pair a Spurs" opens on an ominous note. Recent news stories about diseased beef and warnings about the health hazards of diets high in animal fat have hurt the market for beef, driving down the prices ranchers get for their cattle. After a hard winter and a late spring, a blizzard comes in late May and is followed by flooding, hail, torrential rains, more hail, another snowstorm, and a tornado. Even worse flooding is yet to come when the heavy snow on the mountain tops begins to melt.

Against the promise of impending disaster, Proulx introduces the comically named Car Scrope, who had a brother named Train. An example of "self-ruin" to his neighbors (174), forty-year-old Car is both an object of pity and a major source of humor as his obsessions make him increasingly grotesque. Years earlier, when Car was still a child, his older brother, Train, "died in some terrible and private way in the bathroom" (151), and his grief-stricken and deeply embarrassed parents never told Car what happened. (Though the reader is never told either, the story hints that Train accidently hanged himself while trying to enhance the pleasure of masturbation.) After Train's death Car began to hear the grass on the ranch mocking him in "a kind of hissing snicker" with the words "Best one lost, worst one stays" (152)—a feeling enhanced by young Car's sense that his parents lie to him and keep secrets from him, and his later sense that his father considers him a failure.

Car also comes to associate the sound of the grass with the snicker of his life-long friend John Wrench, who in high school used to sit in the movie theater and invite girls "to have some of his popcorn, his penis thrust through the bottom of the box" (151). Later Wrench became the catalyst for Car's "self-ruin" after Car discovered his wife, Jeri, having sex with his old friend. The seeds for Car's downfall, however, lie far deeper in his psyche, in a strong sense of sexual and social inadequacy fueled by a confused association of sex and death.

After discovering Wrench with Jeri, Car still wanted his marriage to continue. After all, "it was only John Wrench" (160), a man with whom he shared many women in the past; the unmarried Wrench has just "missed the difference between those girls and a wife" (156). When Jeri insisted on a divorce, Car, who was drinking heavily, forced her to ride in his pickup with him to talk things over and nearly killed them both in a serious accident that left him with so many broken bones "that he was now held together with dozens of steel pins, metal plates, and lag screws" (154). After Car got out of the hospital and exacted revenge on Jeri and Wrench by shooting up her car and Wrench's truck, Jeri moved home to South Dakota. Car began to forgive his friend since "baby days," thinking, "Jeri had been Scrope's little South Dakota bird who'd perched a while and flew off, but John Wrench went back to the beginning and one of them would hoist the other's coffin" (156). Later, when Wrench came to apologize to Car for what "was nothing beyond a reflexive deed," the two men got drunk together and decided "that Jeri had caused the trouble and all the sad consequences" (174). Reinforced by other, minor incidents in the story, this episode demonstrates the secondary role of women in an environment where men develop, and must maintain, strong bonds in their battles against the forces of nature. Though some women in the story do fill men's roles, men still see them as merely potential sexual partners.

One woman who is as at home out of doors as most of the men is Inez Muddyman. Car's nearest neighbors, she and her husband, Sutton, have responded to dropping beef prices by turning their ranch, the Box Hammerhandle, into a dude ranch. Running it proves to be "hard work made harder by the need for intense and unremitting cheeriness" (154) while dealing with urban "dudes" with no concept of how to take care of themselves in the country. For example, after one lost guest set a grass fire trying to make smoke signals to attract rescuers, the Muddymans have made a rule that their guests must carry cell phones or "hold onto a long string attached to the porch rail" (169) when they go out for walks.

On a trip to town Sutton buys Inez an expensive, irresistibly beautiful pair of spurs. Their maker is the appropriately named Harold Batts, a former metallurgical engineer, who now belongs to a sect called the Final Daze and believes that the end of the world is near. When he finished this particularly striking pair of spurs, steel shanks "blued to the iridescent flush of ripe plums" and bedecked with silver comets, he commented to his wife's cat that these spurs have "some power," and adds, "Somebody's going to Connect" (158). His words prove prophetic, and—given his millenarian tendency to see signs of the end of the world all about him—the way in which the successive owners of the spurs "connect" might also have been predicted. When Sutton buys the spurs, Batts tells him that they depict the Hale-Bopp comet, which he calls a sign that life on earth is "in the final times": "The position of the earth in space is going to shift. There are forces coming that will make iron swim" (161). Sutton laughs at Batts's prediction, more worried about how to keep Inez from finding out that he has spent all their tax refund, three hundred dollars, on her birthday gift than he is concerned about Batts's warning of impeding doom.

Everyone who sees Inez's new spurs wants them, but no one reacts as strongly as Car Scrope, who has never been attracted to the scrawny redhead and harbors a secret resentment for her because he believes she played a part in Jeri's departure for South Dakota. When she rides her horse to the Coffeepot ranch, where Scrope has been living in slovenly self-pity, to discuss the annual "fake roundup" he usually helps the Muddymans stage for the dudes, the story enters into magical realism. As Car leans over to examine the spurs, he hears in his head a "mixed buzz like radio static" (163), as though all the metal in his body is attracted to the spurs. He immediately develops a terrible headache and a strong sexual desire for the previously unappealing Inez. He makes such coarse and persistent overtures to her that she is forced to push him away and run for her horse. He then keeps trying to find her alone, meeting her once or twice while she is riding. Each time the spurs seem to trigger his longing. When Inez finally asks Sutton to speak to Car, her husband ignores her and talks about the animal, larger than a coyote and probably a dog, that is killing their sheep. Inez remembers how Sutton had once made "a trio" with Scrope and Wrench, "out having themselves a high-heeled old time, the rotten pigs" (169).

The spurs seem to have passed on some of Batts's millenarian thoughts to Inez. On her visit to Scrope she mentioned asking her cleaning woman to vacuum up the box elder bugs infesting the dudes' cabins and said, "Gives me a queasy feelin to hear them bugs rattlin up the hose, no way out. What they must be thinkin—end of the world, I guess" (164).

The end of Inez's world comes one day when she rides out on horseback to find three female dudes from New York who call to say they are lost and have seen wolves. Sure that they have encountered only coyotes, Inez finds the women quickly and points them in the direction of the clearly visible smoke from the ranch chimney. She continues on for a ride alone and finds to her surprise that the dudes have indeed seen a wolf, which is probably the animal killing their sheep. "Without thinking" she lassos the wolf, which frightens her mare so badly that it throws her. She breaks her neck and dies.

CLOSE RANGE: WYOMING STORIES

The wolf escapes and local opinion dismisses the dudes' story "as eastern hysteria" (171), thus combining a whole succession of dudes in a composite modern version of "The Little Boy Who Cried Wolf."

After Inez's funeral, Sutton puts the ranch up for sale and moves to Oregon. The spurs end up in a box of old ropes that Mrs. Freeze, Car's foreman, buys for two dollars at the auction of the Muddymans' goods. Their ranch is sold to an actor named Fane who plays "a Jupiterean warlord in a science-fiction television series" (171). He renames the ranch the Galaxy, stocks it with cutting horses, and hires Texans instead of locals as ranch hands.

Mrs. Freeze, who has worked at the Coffeepot for twenty years, is "a crusty old whipcord who looked like a man, dressed like a man, talked like a man and swore like a man, but carried a bosom shelf, an irritation to her as it got in the way of her roping" (153). Once Car sees her wearing the spurs, however, he has the same reaction to her that he had when he saw Inez wearing them. He feels "the metal plates straining against his skin, the screws pulling out of his bones," and exclaims, "My goddamn brain is blowing up" (179).

Tiring of Car's increasingly forceful advances, Mrs. Freeze quits her job at the Coffeepot and calls Haul Smith, foreman at the Galaxy, who offers her a job in exchange for the spurs. Carr descends further into self-pity: "He couldn't beat the loneliness but the place had its claim on him and there was no leaving unless through his brother's door" (180). With Mrs. Freeze and the spurs gone, "Scrope's hat felt like a plugged-in hot plate on his head," but his headaches "evaporated" (180).

Bad luck continues to follow the owners of the spurs. In the second week of June, after the much-anticipated flooding arrives,

Haul Smith and his horse drown while trying to cross the swollen Big Girl Creek at a ford that is "usable only in early spring and late summer" (154) and has been made all the more treacherous by the breaking of Car's dam, which has been neglected since Mrs. Freeze's departure from the Coffeepot.

Mrs. Freeze survives her ownership of the spurs, but not without some bad luck. Fane loses interest in ranching and sells the Galaxy to "a breakfast food mogul sworn to organically grown grains who said he wanted nothing more than to let the ranch 'revert to a state of nature'" (183). As a result, Mrs. Freeze loses her job.

Haul Smith's boots are never recovered. Several ranch hands have looked for them, hoping to find the spurs, but "the weighted boots had lodged under a sunken steel beam of the old railroad trestle, the spurs seeking sister metal" (183). Even there they continue to exert their influence on Car. He sits by the creek all day long. As his new foreman, Benny Horn, tells Mrs. Freeze, Car "[g]oes down by the old railroad trestle right after breakfast . . . . And he comes back up around dark" (184). Suffering from daily headaches, he even considers pitching a tent by the creek so he can spend the night there, but finds some of the poles are missing. While his ranch is being run by a petty thief of a foreman and a brain-damaged ranch hand, Car stares at the water. Once Benny sees Car sticking his head into the water—no doubt trying to discover what has drawn him to this place.

While Car's obsessions can be partly explained by his mental instability, the physical influence of his injuries, and delusional tendencies that date from childhood, this final obsession is beyond rational explanation. The story ends firmly in the realm of magical realism, with Car reduced by his obsession with the spurs to a grotesque parody of a human being. As the epigraph to *Close Range* points out, "Reality's never been of much use out here."

"A Lonely Coast"

The only story in *Close Range* that is narrated from a first-person perspective, "A Lonely Coast" has deceptively uncomplicated dual plotlines. The first concerns the narrator's gradually unfolding story of how, leaving her husband of nine years after she discovered him having sex with the fifteen-year-old daughter of their hired hand, she went to live in a tiny trailer and began working part time as a waitress and bartender. The second is her description of the downward spiral of Josanna Skiles, who loses her job and is about to lose her boyfriend just as she comes to a violent end. Yet the story is a lyrical analysis of a complex tangle of emotions—loneliness, sexual longing, anger, and jealousy—that, described through vibrant images conveying their intensity, come together in a final outpouring of violence.

Josanna's story is attended by images of fire. The narrator begins by asking, "You ever see a house burning up in the night, way to hell and gone out there on the plains? Nothing but blackness and your headlights cutting a little wedge into it, could be the middle of the ocean for all you can see." She compares Josanna to such a house, which "you could only watch," because she is "too far away" for anyone to save her or even care much about her. Caught up in examining the failure of her marriage, the narrator says she sensed "a feeling of coming heat," but adds, "I didn't have a grip on much" (187).

The narrator's reference to the ocean introduces another series of images, which become associated with her own state of mind. Later she describes the only vacation she and her husband ever took together, a visit to her brother in Oregon. She recalls that, as they stood on a rocky point at dusk, in the fog and cold weather, watching the waves roll into shore, "[u]p the lonely coast a stuttering blink warned ships away" from the rocks (191). When she told her husband they need lighthouses in Wyoming, he responded that "no, what we needed was a wall around the state and turrets with machine guns in them" (191). This passage links the narrator's pervasive loneliness and yearning with the undercurrent of violence that runs through the story. The "lonely coast" is not a place of peace. It is a borderline that marks a point of change, a place where frightening things may happen.

The narrator alludes to the connection between passion and violence as she tries to explain the attraction of women to men with "hair-trigger tempers": "Wyos are touchers, hot-blooded and quick, and physically yearning. Maybe it's because they spend so much time handling livestock, but people here are always handshaking, patting, smooching, caressing, enfolding. This instinct extends to anger, the lightning backhand slap, the hip-shot to throw you off balance, the elbow, a jerk and wrench, the sway, and then the serious stuff that's meant to kill and sometimes does." Josanna is the veteran of a marriage "full of fighting and black eyes" (193), as are Palma and Ruth, the two other divorcées with whom she frequents the Gold Buckle, where the narrator tends bar on the weekends.

Josanna's friends, according to the narrator, are "burning at a slower rate than Josanna, but in their own desperate ways also disintegrating into drifts of ash." Desperate for men in their lives, all three women read personal advertisements in the newspaper and have causal sex with men they pick up in the bar. From the moment she sees Elk Nelson, Josanna is "helpless crazy for him . . . and crazy jealous" (194). Elk tests Josanna constantly, flirting with other women in her presence to see "how far he could shove before she hit the wall" (195).

One hot night in August, as Elk is fondling Palma in the Gold Buckle, Josanna arrives and announces that not only has she had a minor car accident but she has been fired from her job at the Wig-Wag Lodge for no reason. The narrator hears, however, that Josanna was fired because she was caught using cocaine. Faced with few job prospects and a relationship that is clearly failing, Josanna concludes, "Everything I touch falls apart" (199).

Then Elk, Josanna, and three friends leave for Casper, Wyoming, in Josanna's truck, and a strange phenomenon occurs: "a sputtering ball of fire" appears outside against the plate-glass window of the bar, so hot that it cracks the glass before anyone can put it out. In retrospect the narrator sees the fire ball as a omen that Josanna's fire was finally about to reach "uncontrollable conflagration" (187).

As the narrator describes what their approach to Casper must have been like, explaining how the driver encounters the city's lights after hours of traveling through darkness, she returns to the image of the "lonely coast" in a passage that is both lyrical and foreboding, while reminding the reader of the insignificance of humankind in the long passage of geological time:

> And if you've ever been to the lonely coast you've seen
> how the shore rock drops off into the black water and
> how the light on the point is final. Beyond are the old

> rollers coming on for millions of years. It is like that
> here at night but instead of rollers it's wind. But the
> water was here once. You think about how the sea cov-
> ered this place hundreds of millions of years ago, the
> slow evaporation, mud turned to stone. There's nothing
> calm in those thoughts. It isn't finished, it can still tear
> apart.
>
> Nothing is finished. You take your chances. (201)

"Maybe that's how they saw it," thinks the narrator, as they drove
into Casper, "drinking beer and passing a joint, Elk methed out and
driving" (201); but, she admits, "Most things you never know what
happened and why" (205). As she pieces various versions together
later, she concludes that Elk took off in a rage after a pick-up that
cut him off and caused him to run into a stock trailer. Then its
equally angry driver followed Elk. The result was a gun battle in
which one person was wounded, and Elk and Josanna died. None of
the survivors knows who shot whom, but the narrator has an opinion about what happened to Josanna, who was found with her gun
under her body: "I think Josanna seen her chance and taken it.
Friend, it's easier that you think to yield up to the dark impulse"
(205).

Behind this gripping story of passion and rage, loneliness and
despair, is a look at the social conditions that contribute to the characters' emotions. Ranching is becoming less and less profitable, and
other jobs are scarce.

One source of jobs in the narrator's small town is the Wig-Wag
Lodge, where she works two nights a week as a waitress. The
owner, Jimmy Shimazo, is a Japanese American who as a child dur-

ing the Second World War was held with his family in a nearby internment camp. The narrator suggests he bought the Wig-Wag from "some perverse need for animosity which he did find here" (188). Jimmy, in turn, is "a tough one to work for" (189), with a low opinion of the local work ethnic, and the lodge—which serves Japanese food and caters to Japanese tourists, who buy mainly cheap plastic souvenirs in the lodge gift shop—contributes little to the local economy or its social life. The extent to which this situation is common elsewhere in the state is revealed in a comment by the narrator: "They say now the Japs own the whole southwest of the state, refineries, big smoke stacks" (200). The two-way racial animosity underlying her attitudes, as well as Jimmy's hostility, signals another "lonely coast" where the potential for hatred and violence looms.

"The Governors of Wyoming"

Another long story, "The Governors of Wyoming," focuses on Shy Hamp, who finds himself caught between two opposing viewpoints on the important issue of land use, those of the environmental extremist Wade Walls and Shy's childhood friends Hulse and Skipper Birch, who are committed ranchers.

As grotesque a zealot as any of Flannery O'Connor's heretical preachers, Wade Walls is a secular true believer, a man inwardly deformed by his rigid extremism. Even he recognizes that people have to be drunk to like him. Though he is contemptuous of a vast catalogue of industrial environmental disasters and the politicians who allow them to happen in "the deceptively empty landscape" of Nevada (211), Wade's particular crusade is against the cattle ranchers of Wyoming, who graze their herds on public lands. Wade despises "[t]hose subsidized ranchers and their gas-bag cows destroying public range, riparian habitat, wiping out rare plants, trampling stream banks, creating ozone-destroying methane gas, ruining the National Forests that belong to the people, to all of us" (216).

There is truth in what Wade says—as borne out by news reports in recent years about the amount of air pollution created by cows. Yet Wade sees issues in black and white and carries arguments to extremes. Thus, in his mind all domestication of livestock is wrong. He calls it "the single most terrible act the human species ever perpetrated" and warns that unless the practice is stopped the whole earth will become "a harsh, waterless desert" (217).

Wade wants to restore the land to its original state, populated only by wild animals that once claimed it. As for human beings, he says: "I want the ranchers and feedlot operators and processors to go straight to hell. If I ran the west I'd sweep them all way, leave the wind and the grasses to the hands of the gods. Let it be the empty place" (218). Wade is good at proclaiming the rights of "the people" in the abstract, but there is no room for individual human beings in his utopia, undoubtedly because their various and ever-changing opinions are too often at odds with his rigid views.

Near the end of the story the personal motivation behind Wade's story is revealed. Like many of the children of immigrants in *Accordion Crimes,* Wade has changed his name and redefined himself. In the act of destruction, however, his true self emerges: "Wade Walasiewicz, avenging son of an assembly line butcher, his father the head boner inserting his knife in the mouth cavity, trimming ropy veins and bruises from the stiff tongue, cleaving skull to remove the brains and pituitary, shearing the horns away and dead at forty-two from some malignant infection" (243). Again showing his tendency to carry his thinking to logical extremes, Wade sees Wyoming cattle ranchers as the people who initiated the process that created his father's dehumanizing job and caused his early death. Far from a disinterested hero of the environment, he is a man obsessed with a deeply personal mission of revenge.

The ranching practices of Hulse and Skipper Birch offer a solution to the environmental problems caused by cattle that is far less extreme than Wade's plan to rid the land of all people and domesticated animals. A tough-minded, impatient rancher whose enemies consider him a "rank son of a bitch with severe ways" (232), Hulse is nearly as dogmatic in his views as Wade and as passionately committed to keeping the family ranch as Wade is to destroying it: "Hulse stood as thousands of men in the west, braced against the forces bending him, pressing him into a narrow chute. He was in a hurry. He struggled with the semiarid climate, the violent weather, government rules and dense bankers, alien weeds, the quixotic beef market, water problems, ornery fellow ranchers. There was not much give in him. He could make it work if things would clear out of his way" (233). Hulse, however, is more realistic than Wade, and he is portrayed as a loving family man, more capable than Wade of caring about people as individuals.

Hulse's brusque manner also seems to yield somewhat to the softening influence of Skipper, a gentle soul who reads the meditations of the seventeenth-century American poet Edward Taylor to ease the grief caused by the accidental deaths of his two young sons. They suffocated in the trunk of the family car as their parents drove around the ranch looking for them. From the poems of the Puritan clergyman, Skipper derives a belief in "the conjunction of God and Nature" and "the sense of divine order in a chaotic universe. It could not be otherwise" (231).

Hulse and Skipper are employing methods designed to restore grass to bare land and improve water quality by continually moving cattle in small groups so that they do not overgraze one area or spend too much time at one water source. It is an alternative to driving one large herd onto allotted land in the National Forest. This approach is not popular with many other ranchers, not only because it is new but also because it requires additional manpower, old-fashioned cowboys, now scarce. Hulse and Skipper try to convince other ranchers that their methods are necessary for the long-term survival of their way of life, but too many think only in terms of immediate expense.

Hulse is not only more realistic than Wade in his ideas about environmental restoration, he is also more clear-sighted in his vision of what Wyoming would be like without cattle and cattle ranches. He sees signs of this less-than-utopian prospect all around him. The land is not becoming pristine, uninhabited prairie. Ranchers are selling their land to large corporations, which are subdividing the property into building lots and "stockin 'the common land' with tame elks." According to Hulse, "your New West" will be mainly populated by telecommuters who sip "capuccino while they watch the elk" (233–34). Earlier, when Renti, Shy's dilettante sister-in-law, learns that Wade is trying to drive cattle ranchers out of business, she asks if he works for a real-estate company, because "isn't that what it comes down to, cows or subdivisions?" (217). Though she sparks Wade's vehement denial and his description of his unpeopled dream utopia, Renti's words are closer to the truth than either of them imagines.

Shy's wife, Roany, is a successful businesswoman; yet her shop contributes little to the surrounding community. Her main line of merchandise consists of modern versions of old-time western clothing made by two or three local women. She pays them the minimum wage and then charges three hundred dollars for each shirt they make. The customers are wealthy people, not the working ranchers and their hands who wore the original, functional clothing she copies. Her shop also sells "natural" oils, soaps, and potpourris that attract mainly tourists, and "funky stuff nobody needed but that they would buy because it was funky stuff" (219). Shy is surprised that Roany's shop does better than his horse-insurance business, that a well-known rodeo star buys a new shirt from her every month but has no insurance on his horses, which are an essential part of his calf-roping act. Roany takes advantage of the American consumerist mentality, selling people goods they do not need and leaching money away from places where it could be put to better use.

The stiffest criticism in the story, however, is leveled at Roany's husband, Shy Hamp, a man with muddle-headed good intentions that have serious consequences. Shy, who wanted to be a businessman rather than a rancher, has found himself the sole owner of his family ranch after his parents and only sibling were killed in an avalanche. A few weeks after their funeral, he wanders into Wade's lecture on "Bad Beef" and soon becomes a convert to Wade's cause.

Shy sells his herd and gives up eating beef. Once or twice every year he joins Wade in doing "harm where Wade said it would do the most good" (224). Sabotaging ranchers' effort to make a living, Shy and Wade open gates, cut fences, and even kill cattle. Shy has never really thought out the underlying philosophy of Wade's crusade "beyond believing it a kind of good" (239). Shy's life is filled with contradictions that illustrate his lack of understanding. While Wade decries all domestication of livestock and eats no meat, Shy has given up eating beef but still eats buffalo meat. His choice of job is also ironic: he insures the lives of people's horses while he kills their cattle. Furthermore, while he has sold his cattle, he still keeps horses and has leased his land to a sheep rancher. His land is still being grazed. Unlike his neighbors the Birches, he seems indifferent to the condition of his own land while he crusades to "save" grasslands in general.

The Birches work to undo the damage done by their father's generation, but Shy's actions help to perpetuate past abuses. Shy's grandfather was a state legislator, one of the politicians Wade so despises, and Shy, who has inherited the beautiful stone ranch house his grandfather built in 1882, has also unknowingly inherited his grandfather's role in the establishment that still runs the state. By doing nothing constructive to effect change, Shy is upholding the status quo. He remains largely ignorant of Wyoming history even as he perpetuates the exploitive land use it created.

Shy has a personal motive for helping Wade. He sees these actions as "the balance column in the ledger of his own evil doings" (239). Shy is sexually obsessed with thirteen-year-old girls, a perversion that is connected to "a journey in the back of Nikole Angermiller's grandfather's old sedan" when Shy was twelve and Nikole was thirteen (225). On their way home from an outing for a history project, Nikole put her hand on Shy's crotch and stroked his penis until he ejaculated in his shorts. Obsessed with reliving this moment of an excited twelve-year-old's loss of innocence, Shy has been paying to have sex with a thirteen-year-old Shoshone girl, but he also feels deeply ashamed of corrupting the girl. Like Wade and Roany, the "sweet" Shy exploits people for his own ends.

Wade's plans for their present protest activities offers Shy a "test of principles" (241). Always before they have gone to other parts of the state, but this time Wade wants to cut Shy's neighbors' fences. Shy says no at first, but he eventually goes along with Wade's plans, even though he can see their absurdity. Wade wants to cut fences separating public and private lands—an act that will either let cattle onto the public land Wade wants to protect or let the animals back onto private land, returning them to the owners Wade wants to drive out of business. Wade's answer—"It's not so much the logic of the act as the action of the act, the point made" (241)— once again illustrates how far from reality he has strayed.

Just before sunrise Wade and Shy are cutting the Birches' fences when Shy is suddenly shot in the hip. Unfortunately for him, Hulse and Skipper have become concerned about reports of intentionally opened gates, cut fences, and cattle dying from eating plastic baby diapers, and they have decided to take turns spending some nights outdoors on the ranch. As an angry voice from below shouts for them to come down—adding, "I have to come up there you'll come down wearin a bobwire necktie" (255)—Wade runs away, leaving the wounded Shy to face his angry neighbor alone.

Earlier, Shy showed Wade the photographs of Wyoming governors that were given to Shy's grandfather and still hang on a living room wall at the ranch. Wade asked about the significance of one photograph in particular: a picture of Governor Emerson "upside-down high above a large blanket gripped by sixty men in cowboy hats, heads tipped back, watching the man fly up." Shy has guessed that the men holding the blanket are voters, and offered the vague explanation that "I know what it means but I can't explain it" (240). Now, as he waits under the newly risen sun for the arrival of an angry man who has counted Shy among his friends, Shy has a hallucination that brings together the image of the governor tossed in the blanket with that of Nikole's grandfather's sedan. He imagines himself sitting in the backseat and looking up through the roof: "There was Governor Emerson up in the air, past his apogee and falling, sidewise and awkward. It was wonderful how clear it was: you were tossed up and out of the blanket, you rose, you hung in the air, faces grinned or scowled at you, you fell, you hit the blanket and that was it" (245). Implicit in the link between Shy's shameful secret and his realization of the symbolic meaning of the photograph is his final sense that he has not been balancing bad with good. He has betrayed his friends and been betrayed in turn. Realizing that his elaborate balancing act has failed—that, unlike the image of the governor in the photograph, he cannot hang in the air indefinitely—he knows he is about to face the consequences of his actions. The story ends with the line "He got ready to smile at the voters" (245). The reader is left to wonder how much past friendship will count with the angry Hulse Birch.

"55 Miles to the Gas Pump"

A brief vignette, "55 Miles to the Gas Pump," reintroduces the theme of desolation and loneliness in a darkly humorous fable about the extreme behavior of which human beings are capable. A drunken rancher commits suicide by jumping off a cliff, but in a moment of surreal imagination, "before he hits he rises again to the top of the cliff like a cork in a bucket of milk" (249).

After his death his wife cuts a hole through the roof of their house to find out what he has kept locked in the attic for the past twelve years. As she feared, she discovers the corpses of the "paramours" he has kidnapped and murdered, women whose pictures have been published in the newspaper as missing women. The rancher's widow also sees evidence that her husband has been having sex with the corpses, prompting the narrator to comment, "When you live a long way out you make your own fun" (250). Offered in the place of the "moral" in a traditional fable, this understated cynicism leaves the reader with the disquieting sense of the infinite possibilities for human evil ready to rise to the surface again and again "like a cork in a bucket of milk."

"Brokeback Mountain"

The final story in *Close Range* is the tale of a moment in time when two young men *"owned the world and nothing seemed wrong"* (253)—and all the sad hard times that follow. "Brokeback Mountain" won a National Magazine Award through its publication in the 13 October 1997 issue of the *New Yorker* and was later selected for a 1998 O. Henry Short Story Award.

Two high-school dropouts, under twenty and without prospects, Ennis del Mar and Jack Twist meet in 1963, when they take jobs tending a herd of sheep in a summer grazing range on Forest Service land high on Brokeback Mountain. The two young men huddle together for warmth one night and fall easily into a homosexual love affair that continues the rest of the summer. Though Jack takes the passive role in their couplings, it is he who initiates the affair, and though each insists that he is not a homosexual, Jack

seems more experienced that the novice Ennis. They consider themselves "invisible" (260), but when Jack tries to get the same job back
the following summer, the man who hired them turns Jack away,
saying he saw him and Ennis having sex.

One night in August during Jack and Ennis's summer on
Brokeback Mountain, Ennis leaves the sheep untended so that he
can spent the night with Jack, and the animals wander into another
pasture allotment, where they get mixed in with another herd. After
five days in which Ennis and the shepherd of the other herd try to
sort out their flocks, Ennis ends up with the right number of sheep
but knows "the sheep were mixed"—a situation he sees as a "disquieting" metaphor for his feelings about "everything," including no
doubt his sexuality (260). As Ennis and Jack descend the mountain
at the end of the season, "Ennis felt he was in a slow-motion, but
headlong irreversible fall" (261). Though neither man seems fully
aware at that moment of the significance of their summer together,
it proves to be a pivotal point that influences the rest of their lives.

After the two men separate, they do not see one another for four
years. Ennis marries and fathers two daughters, while Jack moves to
Texas, marries a woman with a wealthy father, and has a son. Jack
sparks the renewal of their affair by returning to Wyoming to visit
Ennis. After they rekindle their passion the two men get together
once or twice a year until 1983. They tell their wives they are going
fishing but spend their time together having sex, each time having
"the sense of time flying, never enough time, never enough" (274).

During their first reunion Jack suggests that he and Ennis get a
ranch together, but Ennis says he does not "want a be like them guys
you see around sometimes." He tells Jack about two men who had a
ranch together "down home" and how, when Ennis was nine, his

father took him to see the body of one of the men in a ditch, after he had been beaten to death with a tire iron and had his penis torn off (268). In Ennis's mind there is no way he can be with Jack all the time, and "if you can't fix it you got a stand it" (269). Jack, however, continues to hold out hope that the two of them can be together.

Ennis's wife, Alma, who has always been aware that the relationship between the two men is not just platonic, eventually divorces Ennis. When she tells Ennis she knows what he and Jack really do on their "fishing" trips, he responds angrily that she does not understand at all. He still sees his relationship with Jack as an anomaly, not a sign of his basic sexual orientation.

At the end of what turns out to be their last reunion, in May 1983, however, Ennis becomes aware that although he has never had any male sex partner except Jack, Jack has another male lover. As they argue over Ennis's realization and when they will see one another again, Jack reminds Ennis that they could have had a life together, but since Ennis refuses, their love is based only on their summer on Brokeback Mountain. Unlike Ennis, says Jack, "I can't make it on a couple of high-altitude fucks once or twice a year" (276). Yet for Jack too their relationship is deeper than sexual attraction. He recalls, and would like to relive, a moment during their summer together "when Ennis had come up behind him and pulled him close, the silent embrace satisfying some shared and sexless hunger" (276). Later, he remembers that embrace "as the single moment of artless, charmed happiness in their separate and difficult lives" (277).

Months later Ennis learns that Jack has died. His wife gives Ennis a complicated explanation of how Jack was killed accidentally while changing a tire, but Ennis immediately thinks of another explanation: "they got him with the tire iron" (277), implying that he was killed for his sexual orientation.

Jack's widow explains that, though Jack wanted his ashes scattered on Brokeback Mountain, she has interred half of them in Texas and sent the rest to his parents, thinking the mountain must be near their ranch. When Ennis visits Jack's parents to offer to take the ashes to Brokeback Mountain, it is clear from Jack's father's "angry, knowing expression" (279) that he is aware of his son's homosexuality as well as his relationships with Ennis and the other man.

The father's hard manner reminds Ennis of a story Jack once told him, one that seems to hold a key to Jack's sexuality, particularly for his preference for taking the passive role in relations with Ennis. When Jack was three or four, his father beat the boy severely and then urinated on him because he had dripped urine on the bathroom floor. During this humiliation Jack, who was circumcised, noticed that his father, who was not, "had some extra material that I was missin" and ever after felt "different" (280).

Though Jack's father, who complains that Jack "thought he was too goddamn special to be buried in the family plot" (279), finally decides to bury Jack's ashes there anyway, Ennis leaves the ranch with a part of Jack. Hidden in the closet in Jack's old bedroom he finds a shirt Jack wore on Brokeback Mountain, which still bears dried blood from a nosebleed Ennis had during their last day there. Inside that shirt Jack placed a dirty shirt that belonged to Ennis, "the pair like two skins, one inside the other, two in one" (281).

Ennis hangs the shirts on a nail in his trailer, beneath a postcard photograph of Brokeback Mountain. He begins to dream about Jack as he was during the summer they spent there, "[a]nd he would wake up sometimes in grief, sometimes with the old sense of joy and

CLOSE RANGE: WYOMING STORIES

release; the pillow sometimes wet, sometimes the sheets." Left with a nagging sense that Jack betrayed him, Ennis nonetheless clings to the philosophy he expressed to Jack twenty years earlier: "There was some open space between what he knew and what he tried to believe, but nothing could be done about it, and if you can't fix it you've got to stand it" (283).

While this nonjudgmental story can hardly be said to have a happy ending, it does end the book on a hopeful note. In a collection where most human interaction seems beset by various combinations of alienation, hatred, selfishness, deceit, greed, and outright criminality, "Brokeback Mountain" holds out the possibility of true selfless communion that—at least for a moment—can make all troubles disappear.

CONCLUSION

Though the overall themes of Proulx's fiction have remained consistent, her settings and characters have not. She spends much of her time traveling, stopping to browse at yard sales and secondhand bookstores.[1] Throughout her career she has been fascinated with old photographs, using her perceptions of the faces she sees in them to develop fictional characters. Though she has emphasized that her fiction is heavily based on research, not personal experience, that research includes "four-dimensional observation" as she notes cultural variations, characteristics of landscapes, and distinctive idioms and speech patterns.[2]

In 1992 Proulx told an interviewer that she already had enough books in her head to keep her busy writing for the rest of her life.[3] Since then she has been traveling the world, finding inspiration wherever she turns and storing away what she finds for use in her fiction. In 1999 she wrote that the new millennium "will be for some of us, perhaps all of us, a time of self-examination, a measure of our resilience and ability to fit changing circumstances both as individuals and as the mass of humanity that crowds the earth."[4] Proulx will still be observing how people cope with change and taking in "what I can of the rough, tumbling crowd, the lone walkers and voluble talkers, the high lonesome signers, the messages people write and leave for me to read."[5]

Chapter One: Biography and Background

1. Letter from Proulx to Bruccoli Clark Layman, Inc., 11 November 1996.

2. Proulx, biographical statement in *Reading Group Guide: The Shipping News* (New York: Scribner, n.d. [1996]).

3. Ibid.; "E(dna) Annie Proulx," in *Contemporary Authors Online* (Gale Group, 1999), accessed online 25 May 1999 galenet.gale.com; *Colby College Bookstore—Alumni Books,* accessed online 25 May 1999 www.colby.edu.bookstore/grads/50s/50s.html; "Proulx, E. Annie," in *Current Biography Yearbook 1995,* ed. Judith Graham (New York: H. W. Wilson, 1995), 481.

4. Letter from Proulx to Bruccoli Clark Layman, Inc., 11 November 1996.

5. "An Interview with Annie Proulx," *Missouri Review* 22, no. 2 (1999): 80.

6. Catharine Savage Brosman, "*Les Annales d'Histoire Economique et Sociale,*" in *Dictionary of Twentieth Century Culture: French Culture, 1900–1975,* ed. Brosman (Detroit: Gale, 1995), 9–10.

7. Proulx, biographical statement in *Reading Group Guide: The Shipping News.*

8. Letter from Proulx to Bruccoli Clark Layman, Inc., 11 November 1996.

9. "An Interview with Annie Proulx," 80.

10. Letter from Proulx to Bruccoli Clark Layman, Inc., 11 November 1996.

11. Proulx, *The Gardener's Journal and Record Book* (Emmaus, Pa.: Rodale Press, 1983), 1.

12. Proulx, *Plan and Make Your Own Fences and Gates, Walkways, Walls, and Drives* (Emmaus, Pa.: Rodale Press, 1983), 83.

13. Sybil Steinberg, "E. Annie Proulx: An American Odyssey," *Publishers Weekly* 243 (3 June 1996): 58.

14. Review of *Heart Songs and Other Stories, Publishers Weekly* 234 (19 August 1988): 60; Kenneth Rosen, review of *Heart Songs and Other Stories, New York Times Book Review,* 29 January 1989, 30.

15. Letter from Proulx to Bruccoli Clark Layman, Inc., 11 November 1996.

16. Frederick Busch, "A Desperate Perceptiveness," *Chicago Tribune Books,* 12 January 1992, 1.

17. David Bradley, "A Family Running on Empty," *New York Times Book Review,* 22 March 1992, 7.

18. Letter from Proulx to Karen L. Rood, 21 July 1999.

19. Proulx, biographical statement in *Reading Group Guide: The Shipping News.*

20. Sandra Scofield, "Harbors Of the Heart," *Washington Post Book World,* 1 August 1993, 5.

21. Stephen Jones, "On the coast of misery," *Chicago Tribune Books,* 21 March 1993, 1, 9.

22. Howard Norman, "In Killick-Claw, Everybody Reads The Gammy Bird," *New York Times Book Review,* 4 April 1993, 13.

23. Proulx, "A Note to Readers," in *Reading Group Guide: Accordion Crimes.*

24. "An Interview with Annie Proulx," 88.

25. John Sutherland, "The Long Journey," *New Republic* 215 (7 October 1996): 44–45.

26. Proulx, "A Note to Readers," in *Reading Group Guide: Accordion Crimes.*

27. Christopher Lehmann-Haupt, "Lechery and Loneliness in the Hazardous West," *New York Times,* 12 May 1999, E8; Richard Eder, "Don't Fence Me In," *New York Times Book Review,* 23 May 1999, 8; John Skow, "On Strange Ground," *Time* 153 (17 May 1990): 88.

28. "An Interview with Annie Proulx," 79–80.

29. Ibid., 83–84.

30. Ibid., 88.

Chapter Two: *Heart Songs and Other Stories*

1. Mary Lee Settle, statement on Proulx, *Esquire* 106 (October 1986): 196.

2. Proulx, *Heart Songs and Other Stories,* enlarged edition (New York: Scribners, 1995), 14. Further references, noted parenthetically in the text, are to this edition.

3. Proulx, "Dead Stuff," *Aperture* (Fall 1997): 30.

4. Proulx, "Reliquary," in *Treadwell,* photographs by Andrea Modica (San Francisco: Chronicle Books, 1996), 9.

5. Ibid., 9–10.

6. Proulx, "Dead Stuff," 30.

Chapter Three: *Postcards*

1. Rosemary L. Bray, "'The Reader Writes Most of the Story,'" *New York Times Book Review,* 22 March 1992, 7.

2. "An Interview with Annie Proulx," *Missouri Review,* 22, no. 2 (1999) 84.

3. Proulx, *Postcards* (New York: Scribner, 1992), 17. Further references, noted parenthetically in the text, are to this edition.

4. "An Interview with Annie Proulx," 84.

5. Ibid.

Chapter Four: *The Shipping News*

1. Sandra Scofield, "Harbors Of the Heart," *Washington Post Book World,* 1 August 1993, 5.

2. Proulx, "House Leaning on Wind," *Architectural Digest* 54 (October 1997): 48.

3. Letter from Proulx to Bruccoli Clark Layman, Inc., 11 November 1996.

4. Proulx, biographical statement in *Reading Group Guide: The Shipping News.*

5. Clifford W. Ashley, *The Ashley Book of Knots* (Garden City, N.Y.: Doubleday, 1944); quoted in Proulx, *The Shipping News* (New York: Scribners, 1993). Further references, noted parenthetically in the text, are to this edition.

6. Proulx, "House Leaning on Wind," 48.

7. Ibid., 52.

8. Cyrus Lawrence Day, *Quipus and Witches' Knots: The Role of the Knot in Primitive and Ancient Cultures* (Lawrence: University of Kansas Press, 1967), 70.

9. Letter from Proulx to Bruccoli Clark Layman, Inc., 11 November 1996.

10. Proulx, "House Leaning on Wind," 58.

11. Ibid.

12. Proulx, biographical statement in *Reading Group Guide: The Shipping News.*

Chapter Five: *Accordion Crimes*

1. Proulx, *Accordion Crimes* (New York: Scribner, 1996), 84. Further references, noted parenthetically in the text, are to this edition.

2. Proulx, "A Note to Readers," in *Reading Group Guide: Accordion Crimes.*

3. Graeme Smith, "Annie Proulx's Musicology," *Australian Humanities Review* (September 1996), accessed online, 2 February 1999 www.lib.latrobe.au/AHR/archive/Issue-Sept-1996/Smith.html

4. Robert J. Allison, "Law and Justice," in *American Eras:*

Development of the Industrial United States, 1878–1899, ed. Vincent Tompkins (Detroit: Gale, 1997), 261–63.

5. Manuel H. Peña, *The Texas-Mexican Conjunto: History of a Working-Class Music* (Austin: University of Texas Press, 1985).

6. Proulx, "Inspiration? Head Down the Back Road, and Stop for the Yard Sales," *New York Times,* 10 May 1999, E1.

7. Silvana Siddali, "Lifestyles, Social Trends, and Fashion," in *American Eras: Civil War and Reconstruction, 1850–1877,* ed. Thomas J. Brown (Detroit: Gale, 1997), 278.

Chapter Six: *Close Range: Wyoming Stories*

1. Proulx, *Close Range: Wyoming Stories* (New York: Scribner, 1999), 97. Further references, noted parenthetically in the text, are to this edition.

2, John Updike, introduction to *The Best American Short Stories of the Century,* ed. Updike and Katrina Kenison (Boston and New York: Houghton Mifflin, 1999), xiv.

Conclusion

1. Proulx, "Inspiration? Head Down the Back Road, and Stop for Yard Sales," E2.

2. Ibid., E1.

3. Bray, "The Reader Writes Most of the Story," 7.

4. Proulx, "They Lived to Tell the Tale: How Adventure Stories Keep Us Entertained—and Alive," *New York Times Magazine,* 6 June 1999, 36.

5. Proulx, "Inspiration? Head Down the Back Road, and Stop for Yard Sales," E2.

BIBLIOGRAPHY

Works by Annie Proulx

Books as Author

Making the Best Apple Cider. Charlotte, Vt.: Garden Way, 1980.

Great Grapes: Grow the Best Ever. Charlotte, Vt.: Garden Way, 1980.

Make Your Own Insulated Window Shutters. Charlotte, Vt.: Garden Way, 1981.

"What'll You Take For It?": Back to Barter. Charlotte, Vt.: Garden Way, 1981.

The Gardener's Journal and Record Book. Emmaus, Pa.: Rodale Press, 1983.

Plan and Make Your Own Fences and Gates, Walkways, Walls, and Drives. Emmaus, Pa.: Rodale Press, 1983.

The Fine Art of Salad Gardening. Emmaus, Pa.: Rodale Press, 1985.

The Gourmet Gardener: Growing Choice Fruits and Vegetables with Spectacular Results. New York: Fawcett Columbine, 1987.

Heart Songs and Other Stories. New York: Scribners, 1988; London: Flamingo, 1989. Enlarged edition, New York: Scribners, 1995; London: Fourth Estate, 1995.

Postcards. New York: Scribners, 1992; London: Fourth Estate, 1993.

The Shipping News. New York: Scribners, 1993; London: Fourth Estate, 1994.

Accordion Crimes. New York: Scribner, 1996; London: Fourth Estate, 1996.

Close Range: Wyoming Stories. New York: Scribner, 1999; London: Fourth Estate, 1999.

BIBLIOGRAPHY

Books as Coauthor

Proulx, Annie E., and Lew Nichols. *Sweet and Hard Cider: Making It, Using It, and Enjoying It.* Charlotte, Vt.: Garden Way, 1980.
———. *The Complete Dairy Foods Cookbook.* Emmaus, Pa.: Rodale Press, 1982.

Selected Contributions to Anthologies (Uncollected)

Fiction
"Collector." In *Boats: An Anthology,* edited by David Seybold, 21–34. New York: Grove Weidenfeld, 1990.

Nonfiction
"Somewhere with Sven." In *A Different Angle: Fly Fishing Stories by Women,* edited by Holly Morris, 13–23. Seattle: Seal Press, 1995. Originally published as "You Know You've Been Somewhere When You've Been Somewhere with Sven." *Outside,* December 1993).
"Waking Up." In *The Literary Insomniac: Stories and Essays for Sleepless Nights,* edited by Elyse Cheney and Wendy Hubbert, 49–50. New York: Doubleday, 1996.
Introduction to *The Best American Short Stories 1997.* edited by Proulx and Katrina Kenison, xiii–xvii. Boston and New York: Houghton Mifflin, 1997.

Selected Periodical Publications (Uncollected)

Fiction
"All the Pretty Little Horses." *Seventeen* 23 (June 1964): 142–43, 180, 182, 184.
"The Ugly Room." *Seventeen* 31 (August 1972): 242–43, 288, 290.
"Yellow-Leaves." *Seventeen* 33 (April 1974): 148–49, 164–65.

BIBLIOGRAPHY

"The Yellow Box." *Seventeen* 33 (December 1974): 102–104.

"Turkey Hunting with Vern Snufflock." *Gray's Sporting Journal* 4 (October 1979): 50–51, 53, 55–56.

"The Pickerel as Gothic Cathedral." *Gray's Sporting Journal* 5 (Summer 1980): 11, 13, 15, 17, 19, 21, 23, 25.

"In Rough Country." *Gray's Sporting Journal* 9 (Spring 1984): 18–21, 23, 25, 27–28.

Nonfiction

"North Woods Provender." *Gourmet* 39 (November 1979): 46–47, 86, 88, 90.

"Books on Top." *New York Times,* 26 May 1994, A23.

"House Leaning on Wind." *Architectural Digest* 54 (October 1997): 48, 50, 52, 54, 58, 60.

"Dead Stuff." *Aperture,* Fall 1997, 30–35. Abridged as "Returning Death's Gaze." *Harper's Magazine* 296 (April 1998): 31, 34–35.

"Inspiration? Head Down the Back Road, and Stop for the Yard Sales." *New York Times,* 10 May 1999, E1.

"They Lived to Tell the Tale: How Adventure Stories Keep Us Entertained—and Alive." *New York Times Magazine,* 6 June 1999, 30, 32, 34, 36.

Nonfiction as Coauthor

Proulx, and Lew Nichols. "The Curious, the Bizarre, the Delectable, and the Impossible." *Gray's Sporting Journal* 3 (September 1978): 84–89, 91–96.

Writings about Annie Proulx

Selected Interviews

Blades, John. "Out in the Cold." *Chicago Tribune,* 29 March 1993, V3.

BIBLIOGRAPHY

Bolick, Katie, "Imagination Is Everything." *Atlantic Unbound,* 12 November 1997, accessed online, 11 September 2000 www.the-atlantic.com/issues/archive.atm

Bray, Rosemary L. "The Reader Writes Most of the Story." *New York Times Book Review,* 22 March 1992, 7.

Gerrard, Nicci. "A Gale Force Writer." *Observer* (London), 14 November 1993, 18.

"An Interview with Annie Proulx." *Missouri Review* 22, no. 2 (1999): 79–90. The only reliable interview, according to Proulx.

Paul, Steve. "On Hemingway and His Influence: Conversations with Writers." *Hemingway Review* 18 (Spring 1999): 115–32.

Rimer, Sara. "At Midlife, a Novelist Is Born." *New York Times,* 23 June 1994, C1, C10.

Rocco, Fiammetta. "Annie's Instrument of the Soul." *Telegraph Magazine* (London), 12 October 1996, 46–47, 49, 51.

Skow, John."True (as in Proulx) Grit Wins." *Time* 142 (29 November 1993): 83.

Steinberg, Sybil. "E. Annie Proulx: An American Odyssey." *Publishers Weekly* 243 (3 June 1996): 57–58.

Streitfeld, David. "The Stuff of a Writer." *Washington Post,* 16 November 1993, B1, B6.

Selected Articles

Busch, Frederick. "A Desperate Perceptiveness." *Chicago Tribune Books,* 12 January 1992, 1, 4. A review of *Postcards* and two other first novels by an established fiction writer, who discusses the significance of Proulx's novel in the context of American history.

Bradley, David. "A Family Running on Empty." *New York Times Book Review,* 22 March 1992, 7. A review that places *Postcards* in the context of other novels that have been attempts at the Great American novel (a work of fiction that defines the American experience).

BIBLIOGRAPHY

Dirda, Michael. "New World Symphony." *Washington Post Book World,* 16 June 1996, 1, 8. A review that discusses *Accordion Crimes* as a twentieth-century example of naturalist fiction.

Eder, Richard. "Don't Fence Me In." *New York Times Book Review,* 23 May 1999, 8. A review that includes useful observations on Proulx's use of narrative voice in *Close Range.*

"E(dna) Annie Proulx." *Contemporary Authors Online.* Gale Group, 1999, accessed online 25 May 1999 galenet.gale.com. Biographical information and a discussion of Proulx's career.

"E(dna) Annie Proulx." *Contemporary Literary Criticism Online.* Gale Group, 1999, accessed online 25 May 1999 galenet.gale.com. A useful selection of reviews of Proulx's fiction.

Flavin, Louise. "Quoyle's Quest: Knots and Fragments as Tools of Narration in *The Shipping News.*" *Studies on Contemporary Fiction* 40 (Spring 1999): 239ff. A scholarly article that links the style of the novel to Quoyle's fragmented sense of self and his quest for wholeness.

Jones, Stephen. "On the coast of misery." *Chicago Tribune Books,* 21 March 1993, 1, 9. A review by a writer on Newfoundland history, who discusses *The Shipping News* in terms of its depiction of Newfoundland life.

Norman, Howard. "In Killick-Claw, Everybody Reads the Gammy Bird." *New York Times Book Review,* 4 April 1993, 13. A review that includes a perceptive discussion of Proulx's use of humor in *The Shipping News.*

"Proulx, E. Annie." In *Current Biography Yearbook 1995,* edited by Judith Graham, 481–482. New York: H. W. Wilson, 1995. A brief, sometimes inaccurate discussion of Proulx's life and her first three volumes of fiction.

Shechner, Mark. "Until the Music Stops: Women Novelists in a Post-Feminist Age." *Salmagundi* 113 (Winter 1997), 220–38. A discussion of *Accordion Crimes* and works by Louise Erdrich and Joanna

Scott to support the argument that feminist writers no longer feel obligated to write overtly feminist fiction.

Smith, Graeme. "Annie Proulx's Musicology." *Australian Humanities Review* (September 1996), accessed online 2 February 1999 www.lib.latrobe.au/AHR/archive/Issue-Sept-1996/Smith.html. A brief, useful social history of the accordion illustrated with examples from *Accordion Crimes.*

Sutherland, John. "The Long Journey." *New Republic* 215 (7 October 1996): 44–45. A review that discusses *Accordion Crimes* as an attempt at the Great American Novel.

Updike, John. Introduction to *The Best American Short Stories of the Century,* edited by Updike and Katrina Kenison, xv–xxiv. Boston and New York: Houghton Mifflin, 1999. Includes an established fiction writer's brief but perceptive comments on "The Half-Skinned Steer," a story collected in *Close Range.*

Other Works Consulted

Ashley, Clifford W. *The Ashley Book of Knots.* Garden City, N.Y.: Doubleday, 1944.

Brosman, Catharine Savage, ed. *Dictionary of Twentieth-Century Culture.* Detroit: Gale Research, 1995.

Brown, Thomas J., ed. *American Eras: Civil War and Reconstruction, 1850–1877.* Detroit: Gale Research, 1997.

Day, Cyrus Lawrence. *Quipus and Witches' Knots: The Role of the Knot in Primitive and Ancient Cultures.* Lawrence: University of Kansas Press, 1967.

Peña, Manuel. *The Texas-Mexican Conjunto: History of a Working-Class Music.* Austin: University of Texas Press, 1985.

Story, G. M., W. J. Kirwin, and J. D. A. Widdowson, eds. *Dictionary of Newfoundland English.* Toronto: University of Toronto Press, 1982.

BIBLIOGRAPHY

Tompkins, Vincent, ed. *American Eras: Development of the Industrial United States, 1878–1899.* Detroit: Gale Research, 1997.

INDEX

Page numbers in bold type denote extended discussions of Proulx's works.